THE GOODNESS OF MARRIAGE

SMYTH&
HELWYS

Smyth & Helwys Publishing, Inc.
6316 Peake Road
Macon, Georgia 31210-3960
1-800-747-3016
©2002 by Smyth & Helwys Publishing

Library of Congress Cataloging-in-Publication Data
Biddle, Perry H., 1932-
   The goodness of marriage : a devotional book for newlyweds / by Perry
H. Biddle.
       p.   cm.
   ISBN 1-57312-372-2 (alk. paper)
   1. Spouses—Prayer-books and devotions—English. 2. Young
adults—Prayer-books and devotions—Engish. 3. Marriage—Religious
aspects—Christianity. I. Title.
BV4529.2 .B52 2002
242'.644—dc21
                                                        2002012613

PERRY BIDDLE

the goodness of marriage

A DEVOTIONAL BOOK FOR NEWLYWEDS

REVISED EDITION

SMYTH&HELWYS
PUBLISHING, INCORPORATED   MACON, GEORGIA

For Sue

If equal affection cannot be,
Let the more loving one be me.

—W. H. Auden

contents

III. THIRD WEEK: SHARING GOD'S GIFTS

IV. FOURTH WEEK: LOOKING TO THE FUTURE

V. FURTHER REFLECTIONS ON MARRIAGE

preface to the revised edition

Since 1984, when *The Goodness of Marriage* was first published, it has had three printings with a total sale of 16,000 copies. When the first edition went out of print, I was pleased that Smyth & Helwys would reissue the book. This gave me the opportunity to make revisions and additions I considered important. In light of recent marriage studies and the impact of today's culture, I felt that three areas of marriage needed to be added. In Week Four, I replaced the Conclusion with a devotional concerning spouse abuse. The Conclusion is moved to the end of section V. Because so many more couples both work outside the home, I added a devotional about negotiating chores. The third new devotional addresses remarriage. Finally, money disputes appear to be the greatest cause of divorce. For this reason, I have included a reference list of helpful books on marriage and money.

This revised edition is a reflection of a forty-four year marriage with Sue that now includes a daughter, her husband and his family, and our son and his wife and their two sons. For the first time in a long writing career for me, Sue has put this manuscript into the computer and helped with the writing of the new sections.

Sue and I have found it helpful to participate in marriage enrichment programs for couples. We have also used professional counselors from time to time and found that very helpful. Since I am a minister and was Sue's "pastor" for much of our marriage, it was necessary to get help from other professionals. We found these experiences enabled us to enrich our marriage and to mature as marriage partners. As you begin your marriage I wish for both of you a long, successful, and very happy marriage. Marriages may be made in heaven, but marriages succeed and mature as the husband and wife seek God's will for themselves as individuals and as a couple. May God bless you in this exciting and rewarding life together.

introduction

Getting off to a good start in marriage is crucial! The first year of married life is critical as a couple learns to relate to one another as husband and wife, to share their dreams, goals, and very lives.

The Goodness of Marriage is designed for use in a variety of ways. A couple can use the book in the days prior to marriage as together they think through some of the most important aspects of marriage. It is primarily designed, however, for use by a bride and groom during the first weeks of marriage. I encourage couples to read one devotional each day, preferably together. I hope that husbands and wives will express their own points of view about the issues and will share their experiences as they read together.

This process can help couples get to know where each partner is coming from as they begin to experience married life. They can build deeper trust, which will allow them to "agree to disagree without being disagreeable"!

I hope couples will leave this book lying around their house or apartment and will pick it up from time to time during the first year of marriage. I think the resources mentioned are useful tools for building a successful marriage, and I hope marriage partners will reread chapters and discuss them.

In *The Goodness of Marriage*, I attempt to deal with most of the critical issues of marriage from a prayerful perspective. I hope that these devotionals will be catalysts enabling couples to relate the grace of God more fully to the many challenges of married life. Several themes recur throughout the book, like themes in a piece of music: commitment, communication, friendship, change, love, forgiveness, and the marriage vows. Stress is placed on the blessedness of giving rather than receiving.

In an earlier book now published as *A Marriage Manual,* I stressed the importance of the follow-up ministry to couples after their wedding. While *The Goodness of Marriage* is designed for couples, it will also enable pastors, family members, and friends to strengthen their support of newlyweds in the early months of marriage. This supportive community of faith will gain insight into some of the ways in which they can encourage the newlywed couple.

While couples are often too much in love to hear and comprehend most of what is said in premarital counseling, they are more open to supportive guidance in the months after the wedding as they work out ways of relating to each other. Since communication involves not only words and thoughts but, more importantly, *emotions* and one's very self, I have focused a week of devotionals on this subject. I am convinced that if a wife and husband keep the channels of communication open, they can successfully face the "for better or worse" of the future.

As newlyweds accumulate furniture for their home, I hope they will also gather books for a family library to enrich their marriage. A number of resources are listed in Suggestions for Further Reading. I highly recommend that readers take advantage of programs and resources for building healthy marriages.

Marrying is like setting sail on a beautiful but unknown ocean. May God bless every couple as they embark on this very special and important voyage.

philosophy of a good marriage

1. MADE FOR EACH OTHER

Then the LORD God said, "It is not good that the man should be alone; I will make him a helper as his partner." . . . So the LORD God caused a deep sleep to fall upon the man, and he slept; then he took one of his ribs and closed up its place with flesh. And the rib that the LORD God had taken from the man he made into a woman and brought her to the man. Then the man said, "This at last is bone of my bones and flesh of my flesh; this one shall be called Woman, for out of Man this one was taken." (Genesis 2:18, 21-23)

In this poignant story the writer of Genesis tells the story of every couple: we were made for each other! Husbands and wives on the first day of marriage often have an "aha!" experience as they begin to know and love one another more fully than ever before. Coming together in marriage is finding the missing part of one's life.

In God's divine wisdom, God decided that we should not live alone but in relationship. If we have lived alone until this point we know what it is to be lonely, to feel unfulfilled, to long for a mate with whom we can share our deepest feelings, grandest thoughts, and fondest desires. Now the day has come when our dreams during courtship days have at last come true.

It is sometimes said of a marriage that it was made in heaven. The marriage relationship is created by God and given to human beings. While some marriages do not last, the institution of marriage *was* made in heaven. In spite of drastic changes in society through the ages, marriage has persisted to this day. We enter marriage feeling that God has brought us together, that we were "made for each other," and that we intend to stay together. God has joined us! The marriage ceremony and the vows we make to one another in public express the deep love and commitment that we feel toward each other.

One myth says that man and woman were originally one creature. "It" was divided by the gods. But now, in marriage, the man and woman who correspond to one another are rejoined. As Genesis says, "they become one flesh." They become what someone has called a "we person."

In marriage we find the one who matches us, the one who loves back in response to our love, the one who cares in return for our care, and whose life complements ours in many fascinating ways. Like a ship that has just been launched and now is moving out to sea, so a couple beginning married life moves out into the unknown future with great hope, joy, and love. We now have someone with whom we can talk and share the little daily happenings as well as the deep meaning of life.

We were not made to be alone. While some people choose a single life, they usually find a few friends with whom to share their life. The church family is created by God's spirit and in the "communion of the saints" we find love, forgiveness, and relationship, whether we are married or single. An intense relationship such as marriage needs other people with whom we can share our life and love and who can offer support and care when we need it. Jesus often speaks of the kingdom of God in terms of a marriage feast or a banquet to which we are invited as guests. This is a way of saying that we were not made to be alone but with other human beings. And as we begin the voyage of married life together, we want it to last forever.

As newlyweds, we feel that our relationship is *special.* And indeed it is, for each person is unique. And each marriage of two unique individuals makes a unique "we person." During courtship a man and woman may call the other "special" and may invent a special name for the other to express this. Often these names carry over into marriage and continue through the years, names such as "honey," "sweetheart," "love," etc. Couples learn a language of marriage, both verbal and nonverbal, by which they express this feeling that they are special to each other and that their marriage is special.

For this reason we give thanks to God for our marriage and for each other. As we reflect on our first meeting, on courtship with its strains and misunderstandings as well as joys and excitement, we conclude that we could not have made this relationship on our own. *God brought us together.* We believe that just as God worked to bring us together, God will continue to weave together the strands of our lives into a beautiful tapestry called marriage. God even takes the negatives and failures and pain and incorporates them into a masterpiece of craftsmanship. Now we may see only the "back side" of the tapestry with its knots and mingling of threads, but faith in the providence of God assures us that there is a purpose and meaning and beauty to it all.

On this first day of marriage we suddenly find ourselves alone with each other after the many gatherings with friends and family of recent days and weeks. We have looked forward to this time when we could be alone, just the two of us. And now it has arrived! We remember with joy the shared meals, the gifts received, the assurances of good wishes from friends. The intense social interaction during the recent weeks may have left us in a daze. But now there is time to relax and unwind, time to reflect on God's gift of marriage, and time to be alone together. This is a good beginning for the long voyage ahead.

Prayer

Lord, we thank you for bringing us together. Thank you for creating us for each other and for leading us to this day when we celebrated our love and commitment in a marriage ceremony. Thank you for families and friends who have shared our love and joy and for the larger family joined by our marriage today. We pray through Christ who forgives and loves. Amen.

2. LOVE THAT GROWS

God himself is teaching you to love each other, and you are already extending your love . . . . Yet we urge you to have more and more of this love.

(1 Thessalonians 4:9-10, Phillips)

This love of which I speak is slow to lose patience—it looks for a way of being constructive. It is not possessive: it is neither anxious to impress nor does it cherish inflated ideas of its own importance.

Love has good manners and does not pursue selfish advantage. It is not touchy. . . .

Love knows no limit to its endurance, no end to its trust, no fading of its hope; it can outlast anything. It is, in fact, the one thing that still stands when all else has fallen. (1 Corinthians 13:4-5, 7, Phillips)

Newlyweds so delight in their love for each other that it is difficult to imagine such love growing even deeper and stronger in the days ahead. Yet this is precisely what the Apostle Paul encourages in 1 Thessalonians 4:10: "Yet we urge you to have more and more of this love"—love that develops and takes on reality in day-to-day relationships. Here at the beginning of your marriage is the best time to begin growing in love, love that is expressed in daily good manners and unselfish acts. We need to hear each other say daily "I love you!" I saw the following message on a flower shop marquee: "Do you love me, or do you not? You told me once, but I forgot." We need to reassure our spouse of our love often.

One way to do this is by asking each other, "What would you like for me to do to show how much I care for you?" You may want to write a list of ten to fifteen items to share with your spouse. You may ask each other for clarification. In order to grow in your love for the other you may want to commit yourself to do at least six of the items on your spouse's list each day, regardless of whether your spouse is doing any of those on your list. Here are some suggestions adapted from *Marital Choices* (New York : Norton, 1981) by William J. Lederer:

1. Greet me with a hug and a kiss before we get out of bed in the morning.
2. Look at me and smile.
3. When we sit together, put your arm around me.
4. Call me during the day, and tell me something pleasant.
5. Wash my back when I'm in the shower.
6. Tell me you love me.
7. Hold me at night just before we go to sleep.
8. Hold my hand when we walk down the street.
9. When we're together, end your sentences with "dear" or "honey" or "sweetheart."
10. When we leave home in the morning, give me a hug and kiss.

In our marriage vows we made a commitment to be faithful to each other, to love each other until death parts us, and to take each other "for better or worse, for richer or poorer, in sickness and in health." Emil Brunner has written in *The Divine Imperative* (Philadelphia: The Westminster Press, 1947) that "fidelity is the ethical element which enhances natural love, and only by its means does the natural become personal. It is therefore the only quality which can guarantee the permanence of the marriage relations." When marriage is based only on romantic love, we may fear that it will someday end. But we have vowed to be *faithful* to each other as long as we both shall *live*, rather than as long as we both shall love. Through the marriage vows the feeling of love is absorbed into the personal will. We *will to love*. This will to love is our guarantee to each other, which justifies the venture of a life companionship.

Christian marriage is unique in that it is *committed* marriage. It involves total commitment to each other, without reservations. As we recall the divorces of members of our family and friends we may wonder if such a marriage is possible. God works within marriage to enable us to go on loving in spite of what may come. We have been taught by God's example of love in Jesus Christ. Think again about the words of Paul: "God himself is teaching you to love each other, and you are already extending your love" (1 Thessalonians 4:9).

We have made an exclusive commitment to each other, "forsaking all others," as the marriage ritual says, and "keeping only to her (or him) as long as you both shall live." One of the mysteries of marriage is that it is only through such commitment to one another that we find true freedom in marriage. We find security and acceptance to relate to members of the opposite sex because we have made an exclusive commitment to one another. This commitment is a growing relationship as we renew our pledge to be loving and faithful from day to day.

There is a deep need within each of us to live in a reasonably secure, continuing, one-to-one relationship. Here at the beginning of your marriage you can rejoice and give thanks to God for the commitment you have freely made in your wedding vows to love and be faithful as long as you both shall live.

This commitment is a growing one that matures and deepens through the years. One young man asked his fiancée if she would still love him when he was bald and had a bay window instead of a trim figure! Our lives, like a river, continue to flow and change. We pass through the seasons of life. Whether you are marrying in youth or middle years or older years, there is still growth and change ahead. In each season and with each change our commitment to each other must be made anew. Just as our love for God grows each day, so our love and commitment to one another must grow and be acted out in daily living.

In these early days of marriage we learn what it means to be a "we person" as we become one flesh in marriage. We have lived as an "I" but now we are united in marriage, and this involves always thinking of the other and learning to become more unselfish. As you grow in marriage remember: "Love knows no limit to its endurance, no end to its trust, no fading of its hope; it can outlast anything. It is, in fact, the one thing that still stands when all else has fallen" (1 Corinthians 13:7, Phillips).

Prayer

God of love, teach us to grow in love for you and for each other. Forgive us when we are unloving. We pray through Christ who loves us and showed us the meaning of sacrificial love. Amen.

3. THE GIFT OF FORGIVENESS

Then Peter approached him with the question, "Master, how many times can my brother wrong me and I must forgive him? Would seven times be enough?"
"No," replied Jesus, "not seven times, but seventy times seven!"
(Matthew 18:21-22, Phillips)

Then Jesus said, "Father, forgive them; for they do not know what they are doing." (Luke 23:34, NRSV)

In the popular book and movie *Love Story*, the author, Erich Segal, asserts that "love means not ever having to say you're sorry." But loves *does* mean saying "I'm sorry." It means not only saying it but being willing to repent and change those things that hurt the other person. Love means forgiving one another, not just seven times as Peter suggested would be enough, but again and again and again. Jesus' reply for "seventy times seven" does not mean we are to stop then. God has given us the gift of forgiveness, and we are to continue to forgive one another even beyond seventy times seven.

Someone has said that success in marriage is much more than finding the right person. It is a matter of *being* the right person. Being the right person means being someone who is loving and forgiving. No matter how much we love another person, we cannot avoid hurting each other. We cannot change the other person, but we can forgive him or her and so give the other freedom to change. And we can learn to receive forgiveness after saying "I'm sorry" and asking to be forgiven!

God gives us forgiveness through Christ's death and resurrection. We cannot earn it or deserve it. We can only appropriate what God freely gives. God's forgiveness frees us from bondage to sin, guilt, and fear in order to change and become more like Christ. We are freed to become more loving, generous, and creative people.

Because we experience God's forgiveness as a gift, by the power of God's spirit we can forgive one another. In the Lord's Prayer we ask, "Forgive us our sins as we forgive those who sin against us." Our own forgiveness hinges on our willingness to forgive—to forgive and to forget! *Forgiveness* is one of the secrets to a successful marriage relationship.

An intense personal relationship such as marriage is bound to create tensions and anger that make us do and say things we regret later. "Be angry but do not sin; do not let the sun go down on your anger," says Paul in Ephesians 4:26. The Bible is saying we are to own our feeling of anger, to recognize it, but not to allow it to control us or simmer and grow. We are to cool it before the sun goes down. Many couples find that it is wise and helpful to deal with each day's hurts and anger before going to sleep at night. A time to talk over the day and say "I'm sorry," a time to forgive and be forgiven, is very important for a successful marriage.

One of the things that we don't want in marriages is "gunnysacking," or saving up anger until another day, according to George R. Bach and Peter Wyden, authors of *The Intimate Enemy* (New York: Avon Books, 1970). Gunnysacking takes place when a husband or wife does something that irritates the other but the one irritated doesn't say anything about it right then. Instead the spouse tosses it back into the "sack" and starts carrying it around on his or her back. Then the partner does something and that's it! The partner with the gunnysack of hurts dumps it all out on the table at once. She or he reminds the other of all the hurts going back years into the past. Needless to say, this is a destructive way of dealing with anger and hurts. It's the opposite of forgiving and forgetting.

The word *forgive* is an expanded and empowered form of the verb to *give*. In the early days of marriage we are anxious to give to the other love, joy, and pleasure—and even more, to give ourselves. Forgiveness is an act of self-donation. Forgiveness assumes that the only gift worth giving is the giving of oneself. Doris Donnelly makes the point eloquently in *Learning to Forgive* (New York : Macmillan, 1979):

> The forgiver is asked to put the pain aside (after recognizing it and identifying it), to be other-centered, by looking at the one seeking or in need of forgiveness, and not at his or her own wound. The giver is asked to be generous.

Forgiving and forgetting mean giving the other a new beginning and giving our relationship a new start. If we want this enough we can say, and mean, "I'm sorry."

Forgiveness is the one and only way to break the treacherous cycle of anger, hurt feelings, gunnysacking, and retaliation. In the first days of marriage we form ways of dealing with hurt feelings that are either creative or destructive. To refuse to forgive is to choose the death of all that God loves and makes for our happiness.

The good news of the Christian faith is that the sufferings and death of Christ Jesus make forgiveness possible. God's gift of forgiveness means that our debt against God has been canceled and the slate recording our sins has been wiped clean. This is God's gracious gift to each of us. We receive this gift by faith, by believing that God in Christ has forgiven us.

When we fail to accept God's forgiveness of our guilt, we may try to deflect our guilt by assigning blame to someone else. In *Feelings* (Boston: G. K. Hall, 1979), Willard Gaylin calls this the "hot-potato syndrome." It occurs, for example, when in the course of doing his wife a favor, a man loses his wallet. Instead of taking responsibility for the loss, he chastises his wife: "If you hadn't asked me to get that I wouldn't have lost my wallet." Gaylin also says that this deflection of guilt probably leads to more domestic quarrels than any other emotion. It is much easier to feel anger than guilt.

The crucial nature of dealing with guilt, anger, and hurt feelings day by day rather than gunnysacking them cannot be stressed too much. Forgiveness is God's gracious gift to us, enabling us to begin anew in our covenant with God. Because God has forgiven us, we should forgive our partner and family members.

Forgiveness is not easy. It is one of the most difficult things to give and to receive in marriage. But no one has promised that making a marriage relationship work will be easy. Love works only if we work at it! And working at forgiving and being forgiven is at the heart of a successful marriage. As Doris Donnelly reflects, "In time, those who forgive experience a freedom and peace that is so compelling and true to what it means to be alive and human, that the urge to retaliate lessens, and forgiveness becomes not an occasional deed but a lifestyle." Don't let the sun go down on your anger but begin today the habit of forgiveness.

Prayer
O Lord, forgive me the wounds I have given others I love. Make me quick to see what I have done and willing to say, "I'm sorry. Please forgive me." Amen.

4. THE GOODNESS OF MARRIAGE

Then the LORD God said, "It is not good that the man should be alone; I will make him a helper as his partner." (Genesis 2:18)

So God created humankind in his image, in the image of God he created them; male and female he created them. (Genesis 1:27)

God saw everything that he had made, and indeed, it was very good.

(Genesis 1:31)

Marriage is good because God made it good. In fact, all that God created was *very good* in God's eyes: "God saw all he had made, and indeed it was very good" (Genesis 1:31). The world is so created that marriage is a structure of human life built into it by the creator. We were not made to be alone but to share life with God and other people. We rejoice in the goodness of marriage because it can help answer our cry for companionship on the deepest level.

The Bible paints a delightful picture of God playing the role of father of the bride as he brings Eve to Adam. When Adam sees her for the first time he exclaims: "This at last is bone from my bones, and flesh from my flesh!" (Genesis 2:23). Adam had an "aha!" experience as he recognized Eve. He shared God's view that it was not good to be alone.

Other passages from the Scriptures reinforce this reveling in the goodness of marriage. While written from a male perspective, verses from Proverbs could just as easily be said about a wife finding a godly husband. "He who finds a wife finds a good thing, and obtains favor from the LORD" (18:22). The goodness of marriage is expressed by the author of Proverbs who says, "House and wealth are inherited from parents, but a prudent wife is from the LORD" (19:14). And the well-known passages from the last chapter of Proverbs say of a good wife that "She is far more precious than jewels . . . but a woman who fears the LORD is to be praised" (31:10, 30). Jesus told the disciples, "But from the beginning of creation 'God made them male and female.' . . . So they are no longer two, but one flesh. Therefore what God has joined together, let no one separate" (Mark 10:6, 8-9).

Here at the beginning of married life we would do well to reflect on the goodness of marriage. But at the same time we must recognize that something has happened to marriage and to us who are the partners in marriage. We seem unable to accept God's good gifts such as marriage without corrupting them. Our rebellion against God and disobedience to the command to love the other as we love ourselves mean that we must live in a less then perfect relationship—for we are, indeed, less than perfect people.

The marriage relationship is possible only because God forgives us and by God's grace we can forgive one another. Each day we can make a new beginning. As we repent and ask God's forgiveness for what we have done to distort the goodness of marriage, God is gracious to forgive. As we say we're sorry for what we have done or failed to do to our spouse, we can ask forgiveness, and we can make a new beginning in the relationship. The goodness of marriage does not depend upon our goodness but upon God's creating it good and renewing the relationship by God's grace.

God intends us to live in a "very good" creation and offers us the possibility of love, joy, and wholeness of life. But at the same time we cannot expect our marriage to meet all our needs or fulfill all our goals and dreams. The commandment warns us not to have any other god before the Lord God, and this includes spouse, the marriage relationship, children, and family life. Jesus says, "But strive first for the kingdom of God and his righteousness, and all these things will be given to you as well" (Matthew 6:33). These "things" include food, drink, and clothing—the things necessary for life. Marriage and family life can surely be included in these good gifts God will provide those who seek first God's kingdom. Marriage is good because it provides the possibility of a lifelong relationship of love with another person on the deepest possible level.

The goodness of marriage is distorted when either husband or wife make a little god of the other. To expect the other to meet all our needs for love, meaning, excitement, and companionship is to expect our spouse to play god for us. In the early days of marriage while we are still very much in love and enjoying the honeymoon, we would do well to examine our attitudes and expectations of marriage.

Marriages sometimes go sour and fail not because the husband and wife didn't love each other enough in the beginning, but because they expected too much of each other. Marriage can be overloaded like an electrical circuit in our house, which blows a fuse. Couples of past generations often had extended families of grandparents, uncles, aunts, and cousins to guide and support them on the journey of married life. This relieves some of the stress on the marriage relationship.

Marriage was created good, but when we expect more than it can give we distort and misuse it. We need friendships in the community, church, and workplace as well as the friendship of our spouse. Newlyweds often find that fellowship with other couples of similar age and interests provides mutual support and friendship. Church groups for couples, especially couples in the first months of marriage, can enable them to discover the goodness of marriage as they learn to live as husband and wife.

Prayer

Lord, thank you for creating marriage and for the gift of my partner. Help me to become the right kind of person so that my spouse and I can grow in our relationship and rejoice in the goodness of our marriage. Amen.

5. DISCOVERING NEW JOYS IN MARRIAGE

Rejoice in the wife of your youth. Let her affection fill you at all times with delight, be infatuated always with her love. (Proverbs: 5:18-19, RSV)

. . . and as the bridegroom rejoices over the bride, so shall your God rejoice over you. (Isaiah 62:5)

Rejoice in the Lord always; again I will say, Rejoice. (Philippians 4:4)

Joy and happiness are two things we associate with a good marriage, yet they are very elusive. If we seek them we may not find them, for they are usually serendipitous surprises in marriage. They are gifts from God to those who work at building a creative relationship. The goal of marriage is unity based on faithfulness to our covenant made in the marriage vows.

Each new day of marriage may seem like the dawn of the first day of creation—fresh, beautiful, and filled with goodness and joy. As we reveal ourselves to our marriage partner and discover some unknown facet of our partner, we take new joy in our relationship. In revealing ourselves, we also discover ourselves. As we affirm the other in marriage, we give him or her freedom to grow and change and love.

All of us have experienced the joys of friendship as we have made new friends and nurtured the relationship in shared tasks and leisure activities. We have discovered joy and given joy to our friend. Couples who have been married for a number of years indicate that they consider their spouse their best friend. It may seem a bit strange to think of a wife or husband of a few days as a friend. Certainly she or he is more than a friend! But friendship in a marriage relationship provides marriage a basic working relationship of give and take, sharing joys and sorrows, victories and disappointments, making ourselves vulnerable, and respecting the vulnerability of the other. Through such sharing of life, we discover new joys in marriage. "This is my beloved and this is my friend" (Song of Solomon 5:16).

Couples who have been married forty, fifty, or more years are forever learning new things about each other and taking new delight in their marriage partner. "I never knew that about you!" a wife exclaims. In these early days of marriage the joy of good conversation with each other enables us to deepen our relationship. Our lives unfold to each other like a flower blooming. Each day reveals a new facet of our personalities, like a lovely rose petal shimmering with dew. As we open ourselves to each other, these discoveries bring new joy to our marriage.

One of the sources of joy in marriage is giving and receiving love in sexual union. One of the secrets newlyweds discover is that "it is more blessed to give than to receive" (Acts 20:35) in lovemaking. As we learn to give pleasure and joy to our partner in marriage, we free him or her to give in return. Together we discover new ways to please each other. And we find that there is a deep satisfaction that comes from giving joy to the other.

In the contemporary Lutheran marriage vows, the minister asks the bride and groom: "N. and N., if it is your intention to share with each other your laughter and your tears and all that the years will bring, by your promises bind yourselves now to each other as husband and wife." Joy in marriage comes through sharing our faith in God, through giving ourselves to each other, and through giving ourselves to church and community service. We discover new joys as we share the events of the day with one another in a debriefing around the dinner table. A funny story, a joke, a cartoon all become greater sources of joy as we share them with our marriage partner.

To be able to laugh at ourselves relieves tension and is an indication of maturity. Little things we do or forget to do may seem stupid and we may take them all too seriously. When we back off emotionally, we may find a freedom to laugh at ourselves. Couples collect stories about an anniversary overlooked or a birthday forgotten that they later can laugh about. Sometimes it is either laugh or cry, and laughing may put it all in perspective and be another way of affirming our relationship. We can even laugh later at our hasty efforts to buy a gift and card at the last minute for our spouse's birthday, efforts that were soon discovered!

New joys in marriage come from sharing our interests and hobbies through the years. In the early days of marriage, we share the joys of participating in sports and other leisure activities. There is joy in preparing the apartment or house we will share. Often tasks such as picking out the right piece of furniture or the right color of paint, when shared, can be a source of joy. We may develop skills in house repair and decorating. Greater joy comes more often through the little daily activities we share than through a major celebration.

Leisure time together on vacation is time for sharing ourselves and sharing new joys. The honeymoon, whether brief or lengthy, is just such a time.

When there is a honeymoon, we are relieved of the usual pressures of work in order to enjoy one another.

Sometimes of course, there is no opportunity for a honeymoon, and that leisure time together must be deferred. Couples would do well to plan to spend time apart as well as time together. We need not feel guilty about spending some time alone or with friends apart from our spouse, for there is a joy in reunion and sharing about our activities when we were apart. Some couples plan regular times apart—family visits or business trips or study time or vacation—in order to create "space" in their relationship. Too much togetherness can be oppressive. We need to feel free to share our lives with each other. Each day we can take new joy in the goodness of marriage.

Prayer
Lord, thank you for the gift of joy. Thank you for the new joys we share each day. Help me to give joy to others. Amen.

6. FAITHFULNESS IN MARRIAGE

(Jesus) answered, "Have you not read that the one who made them at the beginning 'made them male and female,' and said, 'For this reason a man shall leave his father and mother and be joined to his wife, and the two shall become one flesh'? So they are no longer two, but one flesh. Therefore what God has joined together, let no one separate." (Matthew 19:4-6)

(Love) bears all things, believes all things, hopes all things, endures all things. Love never ends. . . . And now faith, hope, and love abide, these three; and the greatest of these is love. (1 Corinthians 13:7-8, 13)

A lasting marriage relationship is based on faithfulness to one another. One of the tasks in the early months of marriage is to develop romantic love into a love based on commitment. Such love bears all things, endures all things, and never ends. God works within Christian marriages, giving husbands and wives the power to be faithful to their commitment. God's love never fails. A marriage built on faithfulness to God and our partner in marriage will endure all our faults and temptations and imperfections.

Christ committed himself totally to his followers and promised to be with them always. He has promised that where two or three are gathered in his name, he will be in their midst. This includes the two persons of marriage. God in Christ is faithful to us even when we are unfaithful. He has shown us what it means to love and be hurt by the one who is loved and yet to go on being faithful. The story of God's people in covenant relationship with God has often been compared to a marriage relationship. God's model of faithfulness shows us how we are to live in covenant with each other.

In our marriage vows we pledge our faithfulness to one another in these words or similar ones:

I, _____ take thee, _____, to be my wedded wife (husband), to have and to hold, from this day forward, for better, for worse, for richer, for poorer, in sickness and in health, to love and to cherish, until death do us part, according to God's holy ordinance; and thereto I pledge thee my faith.

The marriage vow is specific in mentioning both good times and trying times in marriage.

We are so much in love at the time of the wedding and in the months that follow that we may be blind to the trials and hardships that affect most lives and marriages. Perhaps you reflected on this with your pastor during your preparation for marriage. Faithfulness in marriage recognizes that the ship of matrimony will pass through storms as well as sail smooth seas. Our commitment to one another to be faithful gives us the courage to continue "till death do us part."

One of the wise church scholars of the twentieth century, Emil Brunner, has pointed out that while marriage springs from love, its stability is based not on love but on *fidelity*. He points out that fidelity is the ethical element that enhances natural love and is the only quality that can insure the permanence of marriage. In *The Divine Imperative*, Brunner states, "Through the marriage vows the feeling of love is absorbed into the personal will; this alone provides the guarantee to the other party which justifies the venture of such a life companionship." Marriage based only on love, says Brunner, is inevitably accompanied by the fear that love may die or fade, thus ending the relationship. But a commitment to be faithful is an act of the will that is permanent.

Christian marriage is marked by our vow to be faithful *exclusively* to the other. Marriage vows often contain the phrase that asks: "Will you, _____, forsaking all others, be faithful to her(him) as long as you both shall live?" We live in an age in which this seems old-fashioned and outdated. But studies of marriage relationships in other cultures and in our own indicate the need human beings have for a reasonably secure, continuing, one-to-one relationship with the marriage partner. God has created us male and female and created the marriage relationship that meets a deep and abiding need God has built into our very nature. We need the security and resultant freedom that come from total faithfulness to one another in marriage. This involves our total being, our mind, body, and spirit.

At whatever age we make this vow to be faithful to the other in marriage, we do it "from this day forward," recognizing it is a continuing commitment. As we pass through various seasons of life, our pledge to be faithful must be made anew. In fact, many couples take the opportunity to renew their vows to one another when they witness a marriage ceremony. As the wedding couple make their vows to one another, the thoughts of couples who witness the ceremony go back to the moment when they, too, pledged to be faithful. Like our love for God, our love for one another needs to be renewed over and over again. It needs to be acted out in every day's activities.

Our faithfulness in marriage should be a growing commitment that matures and deepens over the years. Here at the beginning of marriage we can commit ourselves to work at love in order to make love work. We learn what it means to think as a "we person" instead of an "I person" as the months and years go by. Here in the early days of marriage we would do well to anticipate that God has much to do with us in the days ahead. God has pledged to be faithful to us, and the Spirit seals this in our lives. Although pledging to be faithful involves making ourselves vulnerable, taking risks, and venturing in faith, God will be with us. By God's grace we can be faithful to one another.

Prayer
Gracious God, you have been faithful to us in the past. Give us courage and love to be faithful to one another in our marriage relationship. Amen.

7. SHARING DAILY LIFE

Beloved, let us love one another, because love is from God; everyone who loves is born of God and knows God. (1 John 4:7)

The thing about marriage is that it is so *daily!* We bring to marriage our ideals of what we want our marriage to become. Very soon, however, we find we are married to another flesh-and-blood human being, not to our ideal—and our partner probably has come to the same conclusion! During the honeymoon we may be sheltered from some of the dailiness of marriage as we enjoy leisure activities, meals in lovely settings, and freedom from the demands of work. But sooner or later this ends.

The early days of marriage are times of intertwining our daily lives, like two vines that grow close to one another and yet never merge. We find that as we live together, we must give up some of our freedom in order to share life with another. Our shared daily schedules may call for adjustments to our usual individual activities.

Although it may be difficult to arrange, for some couples a shared meal-time once or twice a day can help them communicate regularly with one another. Mealtime can be a time of recapping the day's activities and planning for the coming days. Real communication—knowing and being known—takes time. Some couples take regular walks together during which they have time to talk over their interests and concerns. Others plan a meal out together each week in a nice setting where they have the leisure to enjoy each other and spend some time in relaxed conversation. Here in the early days of marriage it is good to develop habits in our daily lives that encourage communication.

We have come through a period in American society when good manners and social graces have been downplayed or even discarded. But if the intense personal relationship of marriage is to blossom and grow, we would do well to "learn to practice trivia" as Elizabeth Achtemeier puts it. A wife and mother who has combined family and career, she comments in *The Committed Marriage* (Philadelphia: Westminster Press, 1976):

> It is enormously important in marriage, for example, that a spouse learns to greet his or her mate whenever he or she enters the room, even if the latter has only been gone a few minutes. . . . It is amazing how many couples never really see each other— never note that the other has a cut finger, for example, or never see that the other looks fatigued. If we do not see each other, we really do not care. . . . Couples need to practice in marriage the art of courtesy, the art of recognizing the presence and deeds of the other by the use of good manners.

Simple courtesy in daily life, such as a wife saying "thank you" when a husband pours her coffee, lets him know she sees and appreciates him. We often are much more courteous to strangers than to our spouses!

Doing little things in daily living that show we care about the other builds a more loving relationship. After all, love is not just something we feel but something we express in daily actions. Ruth told her mother-in-law,

Naomi, that she wanted to be a part of her daily living, going where she would go and lodging where she would lodge (Ruth 1:16).

One of the scary and risky things about the dailiness of marriage is making ourselves vulnerable in personal relationships. To say "thank you" and to ask pardon for interruptions, to ask how the other feels and to compliment the other are necessities of a successful marriage. They signal to the other, "I see you and appreciate you as a person. I care about you through my actions."

It is all too easy to get so caught up in working and watching TV and other leisure activities that we fail to have time for each other. Preventive medicine and good health habits can often do far more for good health and long life than a miracle drug or a new surgical technique. The same is even truer of the health of our marriages. Some good daily habits of affirming the other, listening to the other, and sharing our feelings and thoughts can insure good communication over the years.

The adjustment of living with another person on a very personal and intense level each day can be stressful. It is important to recognize the other's need for privacy and time alone. To share the same bed, the same bathroom, and the same house day after day can make one or both partners long for some time just to be alone or with friends apart from our mate.

We need to give each other freedom in daily living to grow and mature. But we also must make time for sharing our feelings and activities. As Elizabeth Achtemeier notes in *The Committed Marriage*: "The sharing of everydayness—that finally is the content of marital communication. It is all the problems, stress, joys, and adventures of living a worthy life in the world." Let us thank God we are privileged to share these early days of marriage with another person who loves us so deeply and upon whom we can heap our love.

Prayer
God, who created us to live each day to the fullest, thank you for this day. Thank you for my partner in marriage. Thank you for the dailiness of the marriage we share. Amen. ❦

communicating

1. DO YOU HEAR ME?

For (God) knows the secrets of the heart. (Psalm 44:21)

Then pay attention to how you listen; . . . (Luke 8:18)

Let me hear what God the LORD will speak, for he will speak peace to his people, to his faithful, to those who turn to him in their hearts. (Psalm 85:8)

Communication is the key to a successful marriage. We are bombarded by words and body language at every turn, so naturally we learn to "tune out" the unimportant. But for a marriage to grow and succeed, husband and wife must work at learning to communicate with each other. Communication, of course, is much more than just hearing words. It involves listening with the "third ear" to what is said between the lines, to the emotional content of the message, and it involves listening to body language as well as to words spoken or written.

Studies of communication reveal that communication is seven percent words, thirty-eight percent tone, and fifty-five percent body language! When all three of these give the same message there is congruence. However, when we tell our spouse we feel great but our face indicates we are in pain, we send a mixed message. No wonder we fail to make ourselves clear to each other when there are so many ways we can send mixed signals instead of congruent messages.

In the early days of marriage we make a special effort to listen to and understand the other. We want to know the other partner in marriage and so we listen carefully, hanging on to every word. We delight in telling the other about ourselves. We reveal not just information, but more importantly, we reveal ourselves and our feelings in good communication. How we see ourselves and how we feel about ourselves is a result of the ways we have communicated with others all our life. Good communication involves getting to know what is going on inside of us and inside our partner.

Communication in marriage is a lifelong process of seeking to know and be known. Love is many things, but basically it is sharing, sharing ourselves. Another word for sharing is *communication*. In marriage we can either be open with one another and share the mysteries of ourselves, or we can withdraw from each other. In *The Secret of Staying in Love* (Niles IL: Argus Communications, 1974), John Powell comments on the crucial importance of communication:

> Communication not only is the lifeblood of love and the guarantee of its growth, but is the very essence of love in practice. Love is sharing and sharing is communication. So when we say that communication is the "secret of staying in love" what we are really saying is that the secret of staying in love is to love, to keep sharing, to keep living out one's commitment. Of course, there is a first "yes," a first commitment made to love, but this first "yes" has an endless number of smaller "yeses" inside it.

Unfortunately, many couples have not learned how to communicate prior to marriage. While they have enjoyed the fun of talking and laughing and excitement while dating, they may have had few serious conversations about their backgrounds, values, and religious beliefs.

When couples begin to experience conflict in their relationship (and it happens sooner or later in all marriages), they usually attribute it to lack of communication. There is a breakdown of communication. By this they mean more than just not hearing the words the other says. They mean a failure to share emotions or feelings. There are two levels of communication in a relationship: *dialogue,* which is the sharing of emotions, and *discussion,* which is the sharing of thoughts, values, and intellectual topics. Couples are initially attracted to each other because they feel comfortable together and are able to share feelings. John Powell points out that "there must be an emotional clearance (dialogue) between two involved partners in a love-relationship before they can safely enter into a deliberation (discussion) about plans, choices, values."And this dialogue forms a basis for discussing almost any topic on which they may agree or disagree. The commitment to one another in marriage includes a commitment to hear the other and to listen with the third ear for the emotional content of the message. Communication does not call for agreement. Our commitment to one another in the marriage covenant is not a commitment to think like the other or agree on everything. Two people who deeply love each other can continue to grow in their affection for each other while holding opposite opinions about many things. However, the longer couples are married, the more they tend to agree on values and other aspects of life together.

Words should build bridges from heart to heart. The words "I love you" spoken by spouses assure one another that the commitment to love continues. Words of affirmation of the other, words of appreciation, and words of thanks build bridges from one heart to the other. We need to speak such words from the heart and receive them in our heart.

One common complaint of marriage partners after a period of months or years is that the other doesn't really *listen* to what is being said. Sometimes a husband or wife tunes out the other as a defense against something they don't want to hear such as criticism or complaining. If we want our message to be heard, we need to couch it in the right way, speak it at the right time and in the context of a shared life. It is important to learn to listen to one another, to build bridges rather than partitions with words and to work for better communication. It's a lifelong task. When we fail to hear the other or when we misunderstand the other, we can ask forgiveness and resolve to make a greater effort in the future to listen to the other.

Prayer
Lord, help me hear what you have to say to me and to us as a couple. Open my heart to hear my spouse more clearly. Forgive me when I don't listen or when I misunderstand. Amen.

2. CLARIFYING COMMUNICATION

Jesus answered him, "Very truly, I tell you, no one can see the kingdom of God without being born from above." Nicodemus said to him, "How can anyone be born after having grown old? Can one enter a second time into the mother's womb and be born?" Jesus answered, "Very truly, I tell you, no one can enter the kingdom of God without being born of water and Spirit." (John 3:3-5)

Jesus' conversation with Nicodemus is a classic example of misunderstanding, creative questioning, and clarifying meaning. All too often we fail to communicate in marriage because we do not make our meaning clear to the other person, or the meaning we assign to words is different from that which the other person assigns to the same words. Jesus used the word *born* to refer to a change of heart, a new birth. But Nicodemus took his words literally and asked what is called a "creative question" to clarify meaning. Jesus replied with a fuller explanation of the meaning of being *born anew* and continues the explanation in the rest of the chapter.

There is a popular quotation that is a marvelous example of what happens in poor communication: "I know that you believe that you understand what you think I said, but I am not sure you realize that what you heard is not what I meant!" One confusing factor in communication is our failure to say what we mean; thus the need to clarify is even greater. Good communication is essential for a successful marriage.

In *Skills for Calling and Caring Ministries* (Nashville: Abingdon Press, 1996), Kenneth J. Mitchell and John S. Savage suggest a number of skills we can learn for more effective listening. In addition to "creative questioning" of the speaker, the listener can paraphrase what the other has said. In so doing we identify with the words by clarifying the content for accuracy. The listener affirms the speaker and lets him or her know what has been heard.

A caring skill that I have found helpful in relationships is called a "perception check." When listening to another person in a serious conversation, the listener responds to the nonverbal signals by making a guess at what the other person is experiencing. (Remember that tone and body language account for ninety-three percent of communication.) An example of a perception check to Sue when she comes in from work breathing a sigh of relief and flops down on the couch is, "I take it you have had a trying day and are feeling exhausted." We need not agree with the other person, but we let him or her know what emotion we perceive is being experienced.

Another useful skill involves describing another's behavior without making accusations or inferences. "Your frowning and gestures with your hands are very evident to me" is an example. A major skill in listening is called "story listening" and involves "identifying the truth (pain or joy) which is told to you through the stories a person shares." Direct "expression of feelings" in which you name your own inner emotional state such as joy, anger, or love is another useful skill. Notice that one can "own" the feeling (of anger, for example) without acting on it. A wife of many years was once asked if she and her husband had ever considered divorce. "Divorce? No," she replied, "but murder many times!" We may *feel* so angry we could strike the other person, but we do not give in to those feelings.

Sometimes we fail to communicate because we get into an argument over some small matter that makes us angry and unable to hear the other person. "Fogging" can be useful at this point. Fogging involves "stating the truth in another person's critical statement." Then you respond only to that which is true for you and not to the whole statement.

"Negative inquiry" involves "coaching another person to constructively criticize you in specifics (rather than generalities)." So a person asks, "You don't like the way the barber cut my hair today?" rather than saying accusingly, "You say you don't like my looks?" We can also listen for the polarities or opposites in a person's story as a way of better understanding the message.

As we get to know each other better in marriage we will find clues through what Mitchell and Savage call "life commandments of listening." Some of the commandments are good; some are bad. We try to listen for the commandments that "drive a person's life and direct a person's behavior." These commandments "are intuitively obeyed and are usually not part of the awareness of the person." Each of us has been taught from childhood certain "rules" to live by: "Clean your plate," "Squeeze the toothpaste from the end of the tube," "Always tell the truth." When we listen for these in our partner, we can better understand how the other is "programmed" and thus understand her or his messages more easily. We can learn where our spouse is "coming from" as we seek to understand one another better.

Practicing the above listening skills is the way to integrate them into our normal conversation and communication, not only with our spouse, but at work and in everyday conversations.

Let me suggest that you spend some time now or at a convenient time later today when you are together practicing these listening skills. They may seem awkward at first, but as you practice, you will get the knack of it. Keep practicing these skills until they become a part of your normal conversation. You will be surprised at how they clarify communication and prevent misunderstanding. Spend ten minutes today in practice, and repeat these skills over the next several days.

Prayer

Holy God who has spoken a clear word of love to us in Jesus Christ, teach us to listen to you and to one another more carefully. Help us to build bridges with words from the heart to the heart of our spouse! Amen.

3. COPING WITH CHANGE

For everything there is a season, and a time for every matter under heaven: a time to be born, and a time to die . . . a time to weep, and a time to laugh; a time to mourn, and a time to dance . . . a time to embrace, and a time to refrain from embracing . . . a time to keep silence, and a time to speak; a time to love, and a time to hate . . . (from Ecclesiastes 3:1-2, 4-8)

"You're not the man I married!" a young wife shouted at her husband. "You're not the woman I married either!" the young husband shouted back. In the marriage vows, couples pledge to be faithful in marriage "for better, for worse." Life is like a flowing stream rather than a stationary rock. A stream is constantly moving and changing its form as it flows on toward a lake or ocean. We never see the same water at that point again—so life flows on and on.

Life can also be compared to a journey. A journey is based on change that we can either resist or welcome. But change we must if we are to grow. Many marriages end because husbands and wives cannot accept the fact that people do change. Our spouse is usually a determining factor in how we change, whether for better or for worse.

Someone has said, "I have stopped trying to become 'grown up' in favor of the process of changing." No one is perfect, and we cannot reach perfection in this life, but we can "press on toward the goal for the prize of the heavenly call of God in Christ Jesus" (Philippians 3:14).

Perhaps before marriage you discussed with your spouse how you think each of you will change and how your relationship will grow in the years ahead. Unfortunately people can grow apart as well as grow closer to one another. If one partner continues his or her education or is in a stimulating job while the other is tied to a dull routine, each partner needs to work even harder at keeping good communication in their marriage. Robert Mason Jr. and Caroline L. Jacobs have this to say about change in their book, *How to Choose the Wrong Marriage Partner and Live Unhappily Ever After* (Atlanta: John Knox Press, 1979):

> For some the resistance to change is so deeply ingrained that acceptance of change, even in someone they dearly love, is almost impossible. However, since it is an indisputable fact of life that people do change, and since this is one of the major reasons listed by couples as the source of problems in marriage, couples would

do well to explore in depth their ability to adjust to the many changes which are inevitable in the years after marriage.

The resistance to change we experience may result from feeling insecure as a person and insecure in the marriage relationship.

Mason and Jacobs point to several "red flags" that indicate potential difficulties in marriage. If you are reading this with your spouse, I suggest you pause and ask yourselves the following questions, which are adapted from their book.

1. Am I locked into a way of thinking or behaving that allows for no difference of opinion or new ideas?
2. Have I made a dogmatic statement about what I want in a partner and do I refuse to tolerate any deviation in this now or in the future?
3. Do I want to grow or do I seem fixed in the status quo?
4. Am I interested in the changes occurring around me daily?
5. Do I get upset easily and act as if the whole day is ruined if things do not go as planned?

The authors point out that if a person is unable to adjust to change before marriage, it is not likely that the person can adjust to change after marriage.

Changing involves taking risks and making oneself vulnerable. The most risky thing in life is letting someone else know who we really are. Our partner in marriage can become our best friend, and like a close friend she or he can hurt us deeply because a friend knows where we are most vulnerable.

Changing one's attitudes, habits, and behavior might be compared to rappelling over a high cliff with only one rope between us and sudden death. Intellectually we know we will be safe, but emotionally it is scary. Our son who was a camp counselor one summer taught me to rappel by going off a thirty-foot training tower and then off an eighty-five-foot cliff! Although I knew I would be safe with two ropes firmly tied to trees and a third safety rope held by the person assisting me, still my palms were sweaty and my heart pounded. Each time I reached the bottom safely, I was exhilarated over making a breakthrough in learning a new sport and overcoming fear.

All of life moves in patterns and cycles, marriage included. Our marriage vows take this into account and purposely include the vicissitudes of life: good times and bad, sickness and health, riches and poverty. What makes the difference between couples who cope with change and weather the storms of life and those who split apart under stress? Two successfully married writers, Ronna Romney and Beppie Harrison, list these factors in *Giving Time a*

Chance (New York: M. Evans, 1983): flexibility, the capacity for unconditional acceptance, determination, the willingness to place your deepest trust in each other. They point out that the most crucial factor is "good old-fashioned unselfishness." There is movement—change and growth—in every marriage that is lasting. You are changing from the courtship and honeymoon routine to day-to-day living. The secret to a good marriage is balancing the rhythms and continuities of marriage with change and newness. The marriage vows catch the thrust of this as we pledge to be faithful and loving "until death do us part" (the continuity) while recognizing marriage involves the changes of "in plenty and in want; in joy and in sorrow; in sickness and in health." In the early weeks of marriage we begin to set patterns of interaction and communication that, if wisely chosen, will build a successful marriage.

There is only one person we can change—the person we see in the mirror each morning! We cannot change our partner's basic personality. God can change us as we allow God's gracious love to work in our lives through repentance and forgiveness. Elizabeth Achtemeier, a successful marriage partner and teacher, writes in *The Committed Marriage*:

> There are lots of differences in marriage that can be overcome by mutual adjustment, growth, and understanding, and above all, by a sense of humor. Human beings can change!—that is the presupposition of the Christian faith. There are also personality and family characteristics that cannot be changed, and there is no point in arguing about them.

Spend a few minutes now sharing with your partner your dreams and goals for your life and your marriage.

Prayer
God grant me the serenity to accept the things I cannot change, courage to change the things I can, and the wisdom to know the difference. Amen. (Adapted from Reinhold Niebuhr)

4. LEARNING TO CARE

Therefore encourage one another and build up each other, as indeed you are doing. (1 Thessalonians 5:11)

Marriage is a school in learning to care deeply for another human being. If we have lived a single life for all our previous years, this is a new experience. If we have been married previously, we can recall how important it is to learn to care for another person. To love another is to care for another, to care for another's feelings and physical and emotional needs.

In the play *A Raisin in the Sun*, Walter tells Ruth, his wife, that the reason for his failure is her failure to build him up and make him feel like somebody, like he can do something. He points out that successful men have wives who build them up. The same can be said of successful women. They have husbands who build them up. Paul encourages the Christians in Thessalonica to "build one another up." Caring for one another's feelings, praising and affirming one another, and giving encouragement is caring love in action. It builds up the other.

Caring for our partner calls for "we" thinking instead of "I" and "me" thinking. This takes time to develop into a habit, but it is basic to a successful marriage. As Ephesians reminds us, learning to care involves being kind to the other person, being tenderhearted, forgiving one another as God has forgiven us. If we have lived all our life thinking first of our own wants and desires, it may take some time of conscious effort to think first of our partner's wants and feelings. Couples who have successful marriages of many years report that they can often anticipate their partner's wants and feelings because they share life so intimately.

One way of learning to care is to start having what Norman Wright in *Seasons of a Marriage* (Ventura CA: Regal Books, 1982) calls "caring days." This was suggested in the first week of this book ("Love That Grows") but cannot be stressed too much. Ask you partner what he or she would like for you to do to show how much you care. The answer should be specific and something that can be done daily. "Please give me a hug and a kiss when we leave for the day and return in the evening" is one example. The caring acts should be positive and should be something only your partner can fulfill.

Studies of behavior modification indicate that human beings respond more easily to affirmation than to criticism. Norman Wright says that the basic principle behind "caring days" is this:

> If couples will increase their positive actions toward each other, they will eventually crowd out and eliminate the negative. . . . In addition, behaving in a loving way will generate a more positive response on the part of the partner and can build feelings of love. By doing this activity you will, first, experience the important "I must change first" principle; second, you will build in yourself and your spouse both self-confidence and other-confidence; and third, you will begin to anticipate improvement in your relationship. Because people anticipate improvement they tend to behave accordingly.

Those who train infants who are delayed in development find that a word of praise, a loving stroke, or a bit of food are much more effective ways to reinforce a new behavior than are angry shouting or physical punishment for undesired behavior.

Holding hands for a brief prayer before each meal is another way of caring. Mealtime should be a happy celebration in which we delight in each other and in God's goodness. This not only makes for a pleasant time but aids digestion! Couples can learn to delay confrontation or criticism until after the meal. We all feel pressures and conflicts, but meals should be times of refreshing body and spirit. When there are children, this special family time together at meals is particularly important for building each other up and affirming family unity.

Learning to care for each other is a way of developing the kind of love needed to stabilize the marriage relationship. Caring concern for the other person is the kind of love that God shows—an unconditional commitment to an imperfect individual. Giving this kind of love takes effort and thought. It means loving the other person as much as you love yourself. Learning to care for each other means heaping love on the other without stopping to consider what one is getting in return. As we put this kind of love into practice, the relationship becomes a truly caring and supportive marriage.

Pause now to consider making tomorrow a "caring day" for each other. If you made a list earlier, review it and see what you would add or remove from your list of things you would like your partner to do on "caring day." If you did not make a list, stop now and make one. Share it with your partner, and ask your partner to do the same.

Prayer

Lord, thank you for caring enough to bring us together and to shower your love upon us. Help us to return your love and to care for one another today and in the days ahead. Amen.

5. DROPPING THE MASK

Let the same mind be in you that was in Christ Jesus, who, though he was in the form of God, did not regard equality with God as something to be exploited, but emptied himself, taking the form of a slave, being born in human likeness. (Philippians 2:5-7)

For (God) knows the secrets of the heart. (Psalm 44:21)

The early days of marriage are exciting and yet threatening times as we drop our mask and get to know our partner better. This will become a lifelong process in communication as we reveal ourselves and learn who this person to whom we are married *really* is. It takes a certain amount of maturity to let someone else know who I am. It takes mutual trust for my partner and me to drop our protective masks of pretending and allow each other to know more about who we really are.

To the extent that people are in full possession of themselves, to the extent they really know who they are, they are able to open themselves to others. Marriage is a school that teaches us about ourselves and our partner. Sometimes it is painful to learn how selfish or unthoughtful we are—or how greedy we are. But the good news of the Christian faith is that God accepts us just as we are, and by God's grace our partner can accept us too.

We must be careful not to rip off the mask our partner wears, but rather give him or her the freedom and space to drop the mask. When we stop trying to get from people what they can't give us, then we can begin to enjoy what they *can* offer. Marriage partners can share whole worlds with each other, but first we must have access to our own internal world. Faith in our own commitment and our partner's commitment to the unity and permanence of marriage gives us the freedom to reveal our innermost being. Faith that our partner loves and believes in us and will respect our vulnerability lets us take the risk of dropping the mask.

The wisdom of revealing our real selves slowly at first is self-evident. We test the cold lake water with a toe before we jump in. "Sharing feelings and thoughts and inner lives can be overdone," says Elizabeth Achtemeier in *The Committed Marriage.* Some spouses seem to feel that they should wear their emotions on their sleeves, that every passing opinion and feeling should be dumped on their mates. Consequently their life together becomes a process of "navel-gazing," of dissecting every minute part of their inner lives.

Dr. Achtemeier confesses that early in their marriage she kept asking her husband what he was thinking and feeling until he called a halt to such introspection. Getting to know each other is a gradual, lifelong process of sharing our daily routine, opening our hearts to our partner in the everyday-ness of marriage.

Actually, self-disclosure is a byproduct of perceiving that our partner is similar to our own self. In a classic study of self-disclosure, *The Transparent Self* (New York: Van Nostrand Reinhold, 1971), Sidney Jourard says that "the similarity which is crucial is similarity in *values*. We disclose ourselves when we are pretty sure that the target-person will evaluate our disclosures and react to them as we do ourselves (within certain limits)." We tend to hide our real selves behind an iron curtain but this curtain melts like wax, says Jourard, when it is exposed to the warm breath of love. This is one of the things that makes marriage so continually exciting and renewing. Within the love relationship, we open our lives to our partner, and we make a jour-ney into the inner space of each other. What we discover is an ever-changing kaleidoscopic world that never ceases to intrigue and fascinate and attract us to each other. There is a mystery about our partner we can never fully know, much less fully understand.

One of the complaints some couples make after several years of mar-riage, however, is that they are bored. This is difficult to anticipate in these first days of marriage and need not happen. *Communication* is the secret to keeping marriage growing and interesting. Boredom results from laziness, not working at the relationship to keep channels of communication open. In *The Secret of Staying in Love,* John Powell says that "communication not only is the lifeblood of love and the guarantee of its growth, but is the very essence of love in practice." He adds that "to the extent that I communicate myself as a person to you and you communicate yourself to me, we share in common the mysteries of ourselves." And, of course, the opposite is true. To the extent that we withdraw from each other and refuse to reveal ourselves to each other, love is diminished.

As we drop our masks we reveal our real selves, not just our likes and dis-likes. When we tell one another our emotions or feelings, we communicate who we really are. We give ourselves. For our marriage to be successful we need to be able to express these innermost thoughts and feelings honestly and openly. To do this we need the assurance they will be listened to, understood, and gladly received. The ultimate expression of knowing and being known in marriage comes through sexual intimacy. The Bible speaks of Adam *knowing* Eve and that, as a result, she conceived and bore a son. We will deal further with this aspect of knowing in the section on sex in marriage.

Many couples have learned from the "Marriage Encounter" movement the value of writing to their partners. Some couples write to each other before marriage. Others see each other daily or call on the phone and write few or no letters. However you may have communicated during courtship, you may find it helpful now to write a "love letter" to your partner and invite her or him to write one to you. The purpose of such a letter is to create an interior life together. We let our loved one know how lovable and worthy of our love he or she is. Love doesn't happen to us. We make it happen! Take ten minutes to put down on paper how you feel about each other. Then share the "love letters" with one another. You may want to do this on a regular basis.

Prayer
Almighty God, thank you for your word to us in Jesus Christ, assuring us you love us even when we are unloving. Help us to reveal ourselves to each other and to respect the privacy and mystery of our partner. Amen.

6. SHARING FEELINGS

For just as the body is one and has many members, and all the members of the body, though many, are one body, so it is with Christ. . . . If one member suffers, all suffer together with it; if one member is honored, all rejoice together with it. (1 Corinthians 12:12, 26)

Good friends share their feelings with each other. We need friends who can understand and accept our feelings of love, anger, joy, and frustration. Our marriage partner should be or become our *best friend.* It may seem strange to call our spouse a friend or even our best friend, but in order to be true lovers, marriage partners need first of all to be *friends.* The lover in the Song of Solomon says of her partner: "This is my beloved and this is my friend" (Song of Solomon 5:16).

A lifetime is usually a long time to spend with another person. Learning to share feelings, learning to *like* as well as to love, learning to give unreservedly of ourselves to our partner is the basis of a successful marriage. Notice that I have avoided the phrase "happy marriage" and have referred to "successful marriage" or "committed marriage" instead. This is because there will be times when we are unhappy, frustrated, and angry in marriage. We may become depressed and even bored. But the marriage can still survive and be a success if we are willing to work at the relationship.

We fall into a trap when we evaluate marriage on the criteria of whether or not it is giving us all the happiness we expect and deserve. We are all affected by what Christopher Lasch calls *The Culture of Narcissism*

(New York: Warner Books,1980). He believes that "to live for the moment is the prevailing passion—to live for yourself, not for your predecessors or posterity." "Narcissism," says Lasch, "appears realistically to represent the best way of coping with the tensions and anxieties of modern life." However, this concentration on self and the cult of personal relations can be disastrous. We live in a consumer economy where all too frequently we expect to get love, satisfaction, security, and personal affirmation like we get food from the supermarket—processed, packaged, and ready for consumption.

The successful marriage is a *shared* life in which one does not take an accountant's approach to the relationship. Marriage is a sharing of deepest feelings, of love and joy, and also frustration, disappointment, and anger. It involves more than giving fifty percent and getting fifty percent, or even giving ninety percent. It may mean giving one hundred ten percent!

We need courage in order to share our feelings. We risk being judged or given advice by our spouse. Many couples, I'm sure you've noticed, are quick to judge one another. One judgment elicits another in a vicious and diabolical circle. All too often we expect our marriage partner to behave exactly as we do, and we are critical when he or she is different. We give advice too quickly rather than really trying to understand the feelings of our partner.

The importance of learning to understand each other in marriage is stressed in a little book by a Swiss physician, Dr. Paul Tournier. He writes in *To Understand Each Other* (Richmond: John Knox Press, 1967):

> If the first condition for the achievement of understanding is the will to understand, the second condition is that of expressing oneself. Every human being needs to express himself ... However, if a person is married, it is toward his wife that his need to express himself is the greatest. In order to express oneself, there must be a feeling of warm and kind receptivity and of attentive listening....
> A great deal of time must be taken in order to build a true marriage. A deep encounter rarely takes place in a few moments. It must be prepared for by hours of careful drawing together.

In order really to understand the feelings of our partner, we need to listen, not to reply. We need to listen long and attentively. A person "needs to feel very deeply loved," says Dr. Tournier, "in order to share an intimate secret charged with emotion."

One of the joys of sharing our feelings in marriage is that we come to know ourselves better. We don't really come to know ourselves through "navel-gazing" or in our diary. Rather, we come to know ourselves in *dia-logue* with another person and in dialogue with God in prayer. Dr. Tournier points out that it is only by expressing our convictions to others that we become really conscious of them. This is why we like to "talk it over" when we face an important decision or are troubled about something. The process of talking to someone allows us to see ourselves and the problem more clearly. Such a confidant should be a person worthy of our trust. When that person is our marriage partner, exciting things can happen, writes Dr. Tournier:

> Marriage then becomes a great adventure, a continuous discovery both of oneself and of one's mate. It becomes a daily broadening of one's horizon, an opportunity of learning something new about life, about human existence, about God. This is why in the beginning of the Bible God says, "It is not good that man should be alone." Man here means the human being. . . . The human being needs fellowship; he needs a partner, a real encounter with others. He needs to understand others, and to sense that others understand him.

To find in our marriage partner a best friend who understands us and with whom we can share our feelings is to find one of the greatest joys of life. It not only enables us to escape loneliness and a sense of emptiness, but it enables us to find fulfillment as we share life at its deepest level with another human being. It is no wonder that marriage has been called a sacrament, a means of grace, in some traditions of the church.

Prayer
Holy God, who understands our deepest feelings, enable us to become more loving and caring of others. Teach us to love not only our marriage partner in a special way, but to love others as we love ourselves. Amen.

7. KNOWING AND BEING KNOWN

But speaking the truth in love, we must grow up in every way into him who is the head, into Christ, . . . (Ephesians 4:15)

[A]nd live in love, as Christ loved us and gave himself up for us, a fragrant offer-ing and sacrifice to God. (Ephesians 5:2)

Several years ago Sue and I went through a career development program that involved taking the Myers-Briggs Type Indicator, a personality profile, to discover our emotional makeup. Some clergy use this or a similar test with couples preparing for marriage to help them better understand and know each other. Each person, like each snowflake, differs from every other one. It is unlikely that nagging, criticizing, or "getting after" people is going to change them. An ancient fable tells of the wager between the sun and the cold north wind as to which could make a man walking along the road take off his heavy overcoat. The north wind tried first, but the more he blew, the tighter the man wrapped the overcoat around himself. Then the sun tried. Within just a few minutes of the sun's beaming down warm rays, the man loosened his coat and soon took it off! In the marriage relationship we may love our partner into changing, but we are not likely to nag her or him into changing.

One of the shocks of the early weeks of marriage is realizing that we are married to someone for life who is different from us and whom we can't change to fit our image of a husband or wife. Individuals often are attracted to and marry their opposites. Studies reveal that even when couples divorce after ten or twenty years of marriage, the odds are they will again be attracted to, and marry, their opposite. Although computerized dating services may match people who are alike, people don't very often choose someone like themselves when left on their own to make the choice. Carl Jung, the psychotherapist, has observed that opposites not only attract but actually fascinate each other. Marrying a person who is our opposite can work out well *if*—and this is the critical point to note—if we do not attempt to change our spouse!

By analyzing the test we had taken and reflecting with a psychotherapist, Sue and I learned, after twenty-four years of marriage, why we relate as we do. We learned to accept the other more fully and realized there is nothing we can do to force the other to change. David Keirsey and Marilyn Bates in their book *Please Understand Me* (Del Mar CA : Prometheus Nemesis Book Co., 1984) offer this insight:

> If you will allow me any of my own wants, or emotions, or
> beliefs, or actions, then you open yourself, so that some day
> these ways of mine might not seem so wrong, and might
> finally appear to you as right—for me. To put up with me
> is the first step to understanding me. Not that you embrace
> my ways as right for you, but that you are no longer

> irritated or disappointed with me for my seeming wayward-
> ness. And in understanding me you might come to prize
> my differences from you, and, far from seeking to change
> me, preserve and even nurture those differences.

In these early days of marriage, we may begin to notice things about our
partner we would like to change. To learn that we cannot change our partner's basic nature, no matter how hard we try, can avoid a lot of frustrating
efforts to do just that. The only person we can change is ourselves, by the
grace of God. And we cannot, short of a conversion experience, make much
change in our basic personality.

The result of taking the Myers-Briggs Type Indicator that Sue and I
found so helpful is that, even in the years after the test, we can look at each
other as a different person. I better appreciate the fact that Sue is someone I
don't quite understand but yet is someone I can, with a sense of puzzlement
perhaps, nevertheless come to appreciate even more in the days ahead. Now,
after years of marriage, Sue and I have come to recognize that personality is
inherent, ingrained, and indelible. We cannot remake our spouse in our own
image, even if we try for the rest of our lives.

But God can enable us to change, and our relationship can change by
God's power. Prayer, reflection on Scripture, and experiences of worship and
Christian fellowship can be channels of God's transforming power. We can
discover what are called "peak" experiences of communication. In *The Secret
of Staying in Love,* John Powell points out that the "occurrence or non-
occurrence of these peak experiences is what make or break a
love-relationship." He describes a peak experience this way:

> First of all, I presume that in such a peak experience one of the
> persons opens himself in such a way that the other is called out of
> himself and out of all his old and fixed positions, out of his old
> calculations, into a new experience. . . . It is the sharing of my
> feelings that will provide you with the opportunity to know me
> in a new way, to know yourself in a new way, and to be changed
> by that knowledge.

Powell goes on to ask why these peak experiences have such a profound
effect. He asserts that "people are transformed by their relationship with
those who are *closest* to them." In marriage we can experience the deepest,

most personal relationship any human being can experience. Powell points out:

> Peak experiences of communication inject a new vitality into these relationships. When you open to me a part of yourself, a reaction, a hurt, a tenderness or a fear that I have never before experienced in you, I no longer take you for granted, or foolishly believe that I know you so completely that I need not look for anything new, as though you will always be the unchangeable you that I first met and loved . . . Change is always slow, but the fact of change and the hope of transformation are very real.

The miracle of communication allows partners in marriage to know and be known. In this process we allow the other the possibility of changing and we may change ourselves. In such peak experiences both partners in marriage are permanently altered because the whole relationship takes on new depth and intensity. I covet for each of you many such peak experiences in the days ahead!

Prayer
Lord, you have broken into our lives and into our relationship with your transforming love again and again. Make us more sensitive to your working in our marriage and more responsive to your gracious love. Amen. ❧

sharing god's gifts

1. SEX IS A GIFT FROM GOD

So God created humankind in his image, in the image of God he created them; male and female he created them. God blessed them, and God said to them, "Be fruitful and multiply, . . . God saw everything that he had made, and indeed, it was very good. (Genesis 1:27-28a, 31)

Therefore a man leaves his father and his mother and clings to his wife, and they become one flesh. (Genesis 2:24)

Sex is good because God created it so. Sex is a gift of God and is a means of fulfilling God's commandment to "be fruitful and multiply." It is also a source of joy and intense pleasure. In the sex act itself a man and woman are united and become "one flesh." In sexual union a wife and husband discover a deeper meaning of loving and being loved. The ecstasy of lovemaking allows us as partners in marriage to experience the "aha!" feeling of at last being reunited with our missing half, as when Adam first saw Eve.

The pleasures of sex are a gift of God and often come as serendipitous gifts from our marriage partner. There is an elusive quality about both sexual pleasures and happiness. To seek it for itself often means to miss it. But when we give love to our partner and keep the channels of communication clear and free in the relationship, then sexual pleasure comes as a gift.

Authorities on marriage tell us that although sex is a gift of God and is a source of joy and expression of love, the successfully married couple who can enjoy each other and delight in each other's company is rather rare. However, it is a goal every newly married couple, of whatever age, strives to achieve.

Sex is more than mere coupling, more than "doing what comes naturally," more than programmed responses to one another's sexual advances. Sidney Jourard defines love "not as an emotion so much as freely expressed behavior, undertaken with the aim of fostering happiness and growth in the person loved." He goes on to say that such a definition may seem grim and joyless and even hard work. In *The Transparent Self*, however, he asserts:

> I would like here to spice this conception with some laughter, some wholesome, lusty, fully expressed, mischievous, lecherous, saucy sex. Not sex as mere coupling, but sex as an expression of *joie-de-vivre*, of a sharing of the good things in life. Sex that is something deeply enjoyed, freely given and taken, with good, deep, soul-shaking climaxes, the kind that make a well-married couple look at each other from time to time, and either wink, or grin, or become humble at the remembrance of joys past and expectant of those yet to be enjoyed.

While sex may not solve anything in marriage, it is "a sensitive index or gauge of a person or of a relationship," says Jourard. Our sexual relationship, like other aspects of marriage, is "for better for worse." Sex is usually the barometer of the relationship, telling us if our marriage is "fair and sunny" or "stormy and overcast."

Because of sin that has corrupted every aspect of human life, including sex, we have too often thought of sex as something dirty, or even evil, to be kept behind closed doors. One of the strange paradoxes in our American culture with its sexual freedom is the prevailing ignorance of the real nature of sex, its physiology, and God's intention for its use. Marriage partners may find it helpful to share their pilgrimage in sex education with each other.

The sexual drive is one of the strong forces in the human being and is often the reason a woman and a man are initially attracted to each other. God's command to Adam and Eve to "be fruitful and multiply" reveals that sex is a very real part of God's good creation and is usually a vital part of every marriage. The law recognizes the critical role of sex in a marriage when it allows for the annulment of a marriage that has not been sexually consummated.

One of the reasons people marry is to have sex within a loving and continuing relationship. We often marry in a romantic haze. We usually "marry" an image of what a husband or wife should be. It can be a real shock to face the reality of being married to a flesh-and-blood human being, not the romantic image of a perfect spouse.

Shortly after a couple is married trouble begins, and it *should!* For as we get to know the traits, needs, and faults of our spouse, we become angry and frustrated. Trouble may begin in bed and be reflected in the sexual relationship. If we fail to appropriate God's good gift of sex and to work at the relationship of marriage, we may find that sex, instead of giving pleasure, is a burden. When we bring to a marriage the attitude that sex is dreadful or disgusting, we need help in working through such attitudes in order to recognize sex for what it is: a good gift from the Creator.

A pastor or marriage counselor can help a couple fully appreciate and appropriate God's good gift of sex. It is difficult to live intimately with another person, to work and share and enjoy oneself and another person, when we are sexually thwarted. In the early days of marriage, it is important for a couple to examine and discuss their own attitudes about sex. They may find release from fears and from ignorance, and they just may have a good laugh together over their misunderstandings about sex.

If there is one place in marriage in which a good sense of humor is a saving grace, it is in regard to sex. Laughing together can give us a new perspective and relieve tensions and frustrations. Laughter is good medicine for marriage at any stage. God must have had a sense of humor to make a giraffe. A little boy seeing a giraffe at the zoo for the first time exclaimed, "I'm not believing what I see!" So too, God must have had a sense of humor when creating sex and giving it to the human race. A certain playfulness and an ability to see the funny side of sex will help us better appropriate God's marvelous gift.

Prayer
Lord, thank you for sex. Thank you for my partner. Help me to laugh at myself and laugh with my partner as we explore our sexual relationship together. Amen.

2. "IT IS MORE BLESSED TO GIVE . . ."

It is more blessed to give than to receive. (Acts 20:35)

Beloved, let us love one another, because love is from God; everyone who loves is born of God and knows God. (1 John 4:7)

The "lost" Beatitude of Jesus found in Acts contains a secret to building a successful marriage: *giving rather than getting.* "For God so loved the world that he gave . . ." (John 3:16). Giving is at the very heart of God and is the nature of love. All too often, however, marriage partners enter the relationship to *get* rather than to *give*. They want to get happiness, to get fulfillment, to get sexual pleasure, to get security. But true happiness, says Jesus, comes from *giving*, not *getting*.

Nowhere is this truer than in the sexual relationship. As we learn to give pleasure to our partner, we get even greater pleasure than seeking pleasure for ourselves alone. The Creator has structured the sexual relationship in such a way that it is in giving of ourselves and giving joy to our partner that we find, in a serendipitous fashion, true joy. The joy of loving and finding our love returned sexually is one of God's special gifts.

The poet Alice Duer Miller has captured the thought in these lines from "The White Cliffs":

> Young and in love—how magical the phrase!
> How magical the fact! Who has not yearned
> Over young lovers when to their amaze
> They fall in love, and find their love returned,
> And the lights brighten, and their eyes are clear
> To see God's image in their common clay.
> Is it the music of the spheres they hear?
> Is it the prelude to that noble play
> The drama of Joined Lives?

Falling in love and finding our love returned is one of the joys we discover in the early days of marriage, a joy that grows as the years go by in a committed marriage.

In the romantic passion of the early days of marriage, it may seem that our partner is overly anxious to please. This is wonderful and we want to keep caring for our partner all through our life together. Marriage is a school in maturing as a person, in learning to give rather than to get.

Poet Bill Matthews has expressed the delicate nature of true love in "The Hands of Loving":

> To hold without crushing,
> To pull without pinching,
> To push without shoving,
> To grasp without clinging,
> That is the handwork of love;
> That is the handwork of love.

To release without reneging,
To loose without losing,
To reach without clutching,
To succour without smothering,
That is the embrace of love;
That is the embrace of love.

To remember without recriminating,
To remind without insisting,
To celebrate without obligation,
To give without receiving,
That is the spirit of love;
That is the spirit of love.

Love can never be described or controlled,
Or limited, or started, or ended.
Love is a gift, freely received, and freely given.
Love is a gift, freely received, and freely given.

Notice the freedom, joy, and mystery that make up real love. "To give without receiving" is another way of phrasing the "lost" Beatitude. Love within the marriage relationship is a gift. We know we haven't earned or deserved such gracious caring and joy. We can only enjoy it and return it. As Bill Matthews puts it, "Love is a gift, freely received, and freely given."

This principle applied to our sexual relationship means that we will refrain from trying to manipulate or use our partner, and we will resist attempts to be used or manipulated. Rape and prostitution can occur within a marriage relationship as well as outside of marriage. Rape involves the misuse of power to sexually assault another. Prostitution involves exchanging sex for things or favors. It cannot be stressed too strongly that neither has a place in a successful marriage. Rather, giving without strings attached, without expecting to get, *giving freely* is the secret of making marriage work.

Sexual problems occur in marriage when marriage partners are not mature enough to give themselves to another, including the intimate, free, and joyful giving in sexual relations. Seldom do sexual problems occur because of a physiological problem. Rather, incompatibility usually results from self-centeredness and immaturity.

Sexual fulfillment does not come from learning the right sexual techniques or mastering as many positions as possible or consistently breaking the national average for frequency of intercourse. Fulfillment comes from learning to give. Such wholehearted giving occurs when we have first known the self-giving love of God in Christ. God's love in Christ frees us from self to live for others, to love others as we love ourselves. There is also an art to *receiving* sexual pleasure and telling our spouse in words and actions what gives us pleasure.

The good news of the Christian faith is that although we fail in loving, although we become anxious and greedy and fail to consider the feelings of our partner, we can be forgiven and can start anew. We can say "I'm sorry," and we can forgive our partner when she or he hurts us. Kissing and making up is one of the greatest joys of marriage. It means a new chance to give to our partner the love we have vowed to give and keep on giving.

Prayer
Oh God, teach me to give and not to count the cost. Help me to give myself generously, body and spirit, to my partner. Amen.

3. MAKING SEX MEAN MORE

The husband should give to his wife her conjugal rights, and likewise the wife to her husband. For the wife does not have authority over her own body, but the husband does; likewise the husband does not have authority over his own body, but the wife does. Do not deprive one another except perhaps by agreement for a set time, to devote yourselves to prayer, and then come together again, so that Satan may not tempt you because of your lack of self-control. (1 Corinthians 7:3-5)

"Sex is great!" you may be thinking in these early days of marriage. As the years go by your pleasure in sexual fulfillment can and should grow even more. As we are able to overcome fears and anxieties about sex, we are freed up to give and receive sexual joy more fully. Sex means more as we are able to trust each other and give ourselves to each other.

There are some guidelines for newlyweds that will enable couples to enjoy each other and their sexual relationship even more in the days and years ahead. David Mace lists five points in *Getting Ready for Marriage*:

1. Check your own sex education to make sure it is adequate.
2. Make sure that your own individual attitudes to sex are sound and healthy.
3. Establish open communication between you about sexual feelings and responses.

4. Insist upon reaching full agreement about whatever sexual experiences you're having together now.
5. Put the emphasis always on sex as experience and not as a performance.

In week two we reflected on the crucial nature of communication in marriage. Communication is particularly important in regard to sex. Remember that nonverbal communication and tone of voice convey so much more than words alone convey. Yet words are important. You should be able to talk with each other freely and without embarrassment about the way you affect each other sexually. Good communication is essential in making sex mean more. Sex means more when there is a spirit of spontaneity and playfulness. While it may be necessary to plan for leisure time together for sex, putting sex on a weekly schedule, like doing the laundry Tuesdays and Saturdays, can make it a chore rather than a joy.

Sex can be more relaxed when couples have discussed their mutual desires for children and agreed on whether or not to use birth control methods. The fear of pregnancy early in one's marriage may reduce the enjoyment of sex. Most couples will have had a physical examination before marriage. Such an examination helps insure that each spouse is in good health and that a mutually agreed upon method of birth control can be used.

Sex means more when there is adequate privacy. If either person has been married previously and there are children in the home, special planning for privacy may be necessary. Locking the bedroom door and disconnecting the telephone can help prevent interruptions.

Personal hygiene can add greatly to the enjoyment of sex. The old saying that "cleanliness is next to godliness" applies especially in marriage. Our personal grooming says much about how we feel about ourselves and those around us.

Sex means more when we see it as part of our total marriage relationship. Sexual intercourse is the way we express most fully our unity as husband and wife. In this gadget-filled society with its emphasis on technology, we may think of sex as something that can be separated from our total life together. Elizabeth Achtemeier comments in *The Committed Marriage*:

> Far too much emphasis has been placed on techniques and performance by popular articles and books. The sexual relation is only one part of the total marital relation. It alone can never carry or preserve the relationship, although it can certainly help. It is a tool that is given for the purpose of expressing the total

relationship between man and wife, but it does express the relationship in a marvelous and joyful way, which adds to the intimacy and appreciation of a husband and wife for each other.

It is helpful for newlyweds to realize that sexual satisfaction is a gradual achievement. The marriage vows don't insure immediate success for both partners in each sexual experience. Couples who have been married for a number of years testify to the growing enjoyment and enrichment of sex over the years. So if there are frustrations and disappointments in these early days of marriage, remember that sexual satisfaction is a process in which husband and wife learn and grow together through the years.

We can make sex mean more as we drop a sense of "ought" and "should" regarding how often sex occurs; whether or not there is mutual orgasm; and whether or not each partner experiences orgasm each time they engage in sex. Sex is an expression of *caring*. It is a way of expressing love and joy to each other. Basic and most important is the giving of ourselves to our spouse in love.

Christ's love is the pattern for our love for each other in marriage. As we learn to give ourselves unselfishly to each other, we will find that sex does mean more. We will learn the deeper meaning of Jesus' Beatitude: "It is more blessed to give than to receive" (Acts 20:35).

Prayer
O God of love, help me to love you more. Help me to love my partner in marriage more and more each day. Let me express my love more freely and joyfully. Amen.

4. SHARING WORK IN AND OUT OF THE HOME

God blessed them, and God said to them, "Be fruitful and multiply, and fill the earth and subdue it; and have dominion over the fish of the sea and over the birds of the air and over every living things that moves upon the earth." (Genesis 1:28)

For you yourselves know how you ought to imitate us; we were not idle when we were with you, and we did not eat anyone's bread without paying for it; but with toil and labor we worked night and day, so that we might not burden any of you. (2 Thessalonians 3:7-8)

But Jesus answered them, "My Father is still working, and I also am working." (John 5:17)

It is becoming more common for both husband and wife to work outside the home. This enables them to enjoy a higher standard of living and greater economic security than they would have if only one spouse worked. In many families both partners *choose* to work rather than being forced to do so for the income. The woman as well as the man is career-oriented and finds fulfillment in her job or profession. Many women are well educated and highly skilled and want to use their professional training.

Work is an integral part of creation. God works and has given men and women work to do in caring for creation and developing human and natural resources for the good of humankind. We often complain about having to work, but without work we may feel unwanted and unfulfilled. Many men and women today are unable to find work and so are frustrated. During the course of a lifetime of work, it is not unusual for a husband or wife to be out of work for a time or to return to school to change careers or be unable to work for health reasons.

For some women, working outside the home and being married at the same time heightens inner tensions since role expectations may be opposite in these two areas of life. Norman Wright examines the potential conflict in *Seasons of a Marriage*:

> For example, what would happen in the career world if the woman was warm, emotional, expressive, noncompetitive, supportive? What would happen in her marriage is she were controlling, pushing, self-assertive, competitive, dominant, etc.? This sometimes happens as it is often difficult for her to shift roles. She has to create two different lives at once! Many decide that it is better to remove themselves from one of these roles. She either quits her job or her marriage.

Pressures on a woman in marriage are much greater than those on a man, says Wright, since men are expected to exhibit the same characteristics in both marriage and job.

Some couples work together in the same family-run business and share life both on the job and at home. When this is the case, it is well for each to have time off to pursue hobbies or sports and develop friendships apart from the shared job. Most couples work in different kinds of jobs and so enjoy sharing with each other the events of the workday. Other couples have the same profession or job but work apart from each other. This can be mutually beneficial as they share ideas and experiences, yet are not with each other at work.

When husband and wife both work outside the home, the couple will need to have clear communication about how the income is to be spent. If the woman earns more than the man, she may need to be especially sensitive to his feelings about the money. If the man is happily employed while the wife is temporarily out of work, this situation also calls for mutual understanding and support.

If the woman chooses not to work outside the home, she should not feel less important and less needed than the employed wife. Being a housewife and mother is a very demanding and socially important role. Some women choose to work part-time while children are young and so are able to give more time to family while keeping a career going.

One of the biggest problems for two-career families is who does the housework. When there are children old enough to help, housework should be a family chore in which all members share tasks. When there are just husband and wife and both work outside the home, there should be a negotiated division of labor.

Norman Wright cites some of the pros and cons of working wives and husbands:

> A husband committed to his wife cares and encourages her and is more likely to share household duties. But most men do not become that involved at home with or without children. The stress of shuffling chores may be more than he expected. If the husband refuses to help, resentment and distance soon appear in their relationship and they begin to reinforce each other in a negative manner. . . . The husband's desire as to whether she remains a housewife or is employed outside the home is a major factor. If he approves there is likely to be higher marital adjustment than if he disapproves.

Sue and I discovered that when she took a full-time job outside the home, marriage became a greater challenge than before. To maintain a close, loving marriage takes good communication and constant effort. Tempers may flare when one or the other feels "put upon" or resents having to work both outside and inside the home.

If one spouse cooks supper in the evening, then it is only fair that the other cleans up and washes dishes. One may take responsibility for doing the laundry, while another does dusting and vacuuming. A simple chart with chores and a checklist can help make it go easier, especially when there are children to supervise in doing chores. Chores may be shifted from time to time. A key to making it all go easier is to heap praise on the person who does a job well and to withhold criticism as much as possible!

Prayer
Lord, thank you for work to do. Thank you for shared work in making a home. Help me to walk in my spouse's shoes from time to time and so better understand what she or he is experiencing. Help me to be more understanding and caring. Amen.

5. MANAGING MONEY

But those who want to be rich fall into temptation and are trapped by many senseless and harmful desires that plunge people into ruin and destruction. For the love of money is a root of all kinds of evil, and in their eagerness to be rich some have wandered away from the faith and pierced themselves with many pains. (1 Timothy 6:9-10)

Money can either enable us to grow together as a couple or can become a wedge driving us apart. Money has such great power because it is *coined personality*. It is our time and energy and talents reduced to dollars. Notice that the Bible says that "the love of money," not money itself, "is the root of all evil." The love of money makes us greedy. Money can easily become a false god to whom we sacrifice ourselves and those we love.

Money properly managed, however, can be a useful servant. It can enable us to buy what we need or want, save for the future, and give to others. When we allow money to become our master, it is a cruel taskmaster. The misuse of money and credit can create a chaos of marriage and severely damage a loving relationship. The key to success in managing our money is communication and negotiation.

Recent research indicates that engaged couples seem to be almost completely unaware of potential differences over the use of money. When divorced persons were asked about issues of money in their former marriages, fifty percent said they frequently or always disagreed about money and its use. Couples undergoing marriage counseling reveal that only eight percent have full agreement on finances while forty percent indicate frequent or total disagreement over money. Fifty-three percent of the successfully married couples interviewed indicated that they agreed on money matters and only twenty-five percent occasionally disagreed. These statistics reveal that money plays a critical role in the success and happiness of a marriage relationship.

Research indicates that *money* rather than sexual adjustment, in-laws, religion, jobs, or other matters is the chief source of marital problems.

While some couples in the past built a successful marriage in which the husband or the wife managed the couple's finances alone with little input or consultation from the other partner, this has changed in recent years. The women's liberation movement and the greater number of wives in the workplace, plus a growing sense of democracy in American society, have combined to make money management a shared role in marriage. One of the secrets to building a successful marriage is to share the management of family finances. Engaged couples find that planning a joint budget and planning for housing, furniture, etc. can identify issues that may become sources of conflict. Some ministers ask couples preparing for marriage to work out their budget and to place a value from one to ten on the various budget items such as food, insurance, and housing as a process to identify potential problems in money management before they become too serious.

Often young married couples feel that it would mean conceding defeat to admit that they differ greatly on economic values. For the first months or years of marriage they may try to keep on believing that they agree, or should agree, on everything. But learning "to agree to disagree without being disagreeable" is important in money management as well as in other aspects of marriage. In *Building a Successful Marriage* (Englewood Cliffs NJ: Prentice-Hall, 1973), Judson and Mary Landis write:

> It is far better for the couple at marriage to recognize that almost surely they will differ on some matters but to agree that they will discuss differences as they arise in order to arrive at working arrangements as early as possible. The time to talk things over is when any difference in viewpoints becomes evident, before the situation reaches an explosive point.

One cannot overemphasize the importance of talking over financial decisions *before* the situation becomes explosive. For example, when major purchases are to be made it is wise to discuss the options together, looking at the pros and cons of each. "Sleeping on a decision" is also valuable since it can prevent hasty, impulsive, and often unwise financial decisions.

While the decisions regarding money management should be shared, it is usually necessary for one or the other marriage partner to be chiefly responsible for paying the bills and keeping the checkbook balanced. Which one takes this chore may depend upon circumstances. Often one partner has the knack for this important task. Sometimes couples pass the responsibility from one to the other after a few years. Many men today, in contrast to the past, appreciate their wives taking a major responsibility in this area. Many couples have a joint checking account and both use their judgment in routine spending. It can be helpful for each partner to have an "allowance" that is his or hers to spend without being accountable to the other partner.

It is sometimes difficult to work out a smooth money management system in the first years of marriage. After a couple have lived together for several years, however, they usually reach an agreement on financial planning and spending. They learn to trust the judgment of each other. Sue and I have found this to be true over the years of our marriage.

It is critical to understand where each spouse is coming from in money management. To understand the other partner's views and feelings about financial matters is extremely important. Let me suggest that you talk over the approach you will use in managing money. Negotiate with each other and keep the channels of communication open. A written plan for spending money that is reviewed and changed as needed can be a helpful tool. One need not be a slave to a budget. Rather, a budget should be a tool that a person or couple uses in order to achieve certain goals in life. Money, when properly managed, can serve to smooth the path rather than provoke family battles.

Prayer
Creator God, thank you for money. Thank you for our shared lives. Help us to manage money wisely. Help us to make money our servant, not our master. Amen.

6. SPENDING MONEY TOGETHER

No one can be slave of two masters: he will either hate the first and love the second, or treat the first with respect and the second with scorn. You cannot be the slave of both God and of money. (Matthew 6:24, JB)

That is why I am telling you not to worry about your life and what you are to eat, not about your body and how you are to clothe it. Surely life means more than food, and the body more than clothing! . . . Set your hearts on his kingdom first, and on his righteousness, and all these other things will be given you as well. (Matthew 6:25, 33, JB)

No matter how much money we earn we will never have enough to cover all our wants. The more income we have, the greater are our desires. If we want something badly enough, we will sacrifice other things for it. A budget is a plan for spending our money so that we make it our servant and not let it become our master. Putting God first in our life will insure that God, not money, is our master.

If you have had a budget as a single person, you know the value of developing a plan for spending. Now, as a couple, you will find a plan even more important since there are two people involved. A budget should be a simple, flexible financial outline to help you achieve your goals. Your budget as a couple will be uniquely your own. It will reflect your individual and family goals and priorities. You should work on it together. Your budget should not be a straight jacket, but a plan to help you spend your money and live within your means. Your budget should allow some money for each person to spend as they wish. Finally, your budget and record-keeping should be simple. Don't try to be too technical or restrictive. Money is earned to be used. While it may seem you have little control over many of your expenditures, a budget will be a roadmap to help you chart your course and to check on where your money is being spent.

You are already ahead of the game if as a couple you talked about money before marriage and worked out a financial plan. If you have not, take some time today or very soon to discuss your attitudes on spending money. An exercise at the end of today's devotional will help in this. Try to discover the points where you agree and disagree. It is important to do this *before* problems in finances arise.

One of the secrets to developing a budget and to solving differences in money matters is to pick the right time to discuss such matters. As I was planning to write this section, I asked Sue for hints and she underlined the importance of *timing* in discussing finances. Pick a time—you may need to schedule it several days in advance—when you are both rested and can give your attention to the matter. (If there are children involved from a previous marriage, you should use discretion as to the extent they should become involved. Working on the family budget can be good preparation for your children for their own marriages!) You may need to do some reading on family budgeting and spend several sessions together working out the plan that meets your particular needs and goals as a couple or as a family. Courses on family finances can be helpful.

A budget should never be used as a weapon to try to force a partner to refrain from spending money. Rather, it should be a mutually agreed upon plan based on projected income the family will have and the expense items to be anticipated. If at all possible, the budget should include provisions for saving part of the family's income. And the single most important item to be in your spending plan is what to give to your church and charities. Starting your married life by giving back a portion of the money God has entrusted to you is the best way to insure wise use of your money as well as having your priorities in the right order.

Attempting to follow a budget that is too rigid can increase tension in marriage. Remember, it is *your* plan and should remain flexible and responsible to your needs, wants, and goals as a couple. The most important point is that you try to understand each other's viewpoints and feelings and then work together to achieve as much agreement as possible in spending your money.

Take some time now or schedule a time with your partner in the next day or so to work together on an exercise in budgeting. Since this is not your actual budget, you can be more relaxed and play with the findings. The process should help you shape your real budget or revise your present budget.

You should each take a separate sheet of paper and write a scale of one to ten across the top of the page, letting one be the lowest and ten your top priority. Next, list the twenty most important items in your spending and give each a value from one to ten, based on your honest feeling about that item. If eating regularly is a high priority then give food a ten! If belonging to an expensive club is a low priority, give it a one or two. Be sure to include savings, gifts, and contributions to church and charities. When you have finished, compare your ratings. Let this be the catalyst for revising or working up a budget. You may want to keep your ratings for future reference.

Prayer
Help me, O Lord, to make you, not money, my master. May our shared plan for spending reflect our faith in you and our obedience to the commandment to love our neighbor as ourselves. Help me see my partner's point of view as we plan our budget and spend our money. Amen.

7. BUILDING A CHRISTIAN HOME

And looking at those who sat around him, he said, "Here are my mother and my brothers! Whoever does the will of God is my brother and sister and mother." (Mark 3:34-35)

As God's chosen ones, holy and beloved, clothe yourselves with compassion, kindness, humility, meekness, and patience. Bear with one another and, if anyone has a complaint against another, forgive each other; just as the Lord has forgiven you,

so you also must forgive. Above all, clothe yourselves with love, which binds every-
thing together in perfect harmony. (Colossians 3:12-14)

When Christians marry they form a new unit of society and begin a
Christian family. Jesus has promised: "For where two or three are gathered in
my name, I am there among them" (Matthew 18:20). In one sense there is
no such animal as a "Christian home" or "Christian family" but only
Christians who live in a family relationship. However, there are distinguishing characteristics of such families. The central one, of course, is that *Christ
is the honored guest* in such a home. He has promised to be where two or
three are gathered in his name.

A Christian family is bound together by steadfast love. As Paul writes to
the church at Colossae, "And above all, clothe yourselves with love, which
binds everything together in perfect harmony" (Colossians 3:14). Love is *the*
ingredient in every Christian family that flavors everything the family does.
Love like the love God has for us in Christ enables us to forgive one another
and begin anew in family living.

Building a Christian home involves daily working at putting love into
practice in our relationships. Faith in God and God's love enables us to love
one another even when the other seems unlovable. In *Christians in Families*
(Richmond VA: CLC Press, 1964), Roy Fairchild has this to say about family
life as Christians:

> It is the Christian faith that whatever help we have is not turning
> our backs upon the unpleasant features of family life but in con-
> fronting the terror of our condition. Otherwise we deceive
> ourselves and fail to realize that *the Gospel is good news for our
> actual existence in the family.* The Bible does not approach the
> family as a place where the Kingdom of God can be more easily
> realized than anywhere else. For here the deepest hurts as well as
> the deepest healing can come; here we both enjoy and are
> damned by our relationships. No, the family has no special grace
> at its disposal that Christ's men or women, single or married,
> cannot have.

Fairchild points out that the simplest misunderstanding is that if two people
are married by a clergyperson and by saying their vows in church, the result
is a "Christian marriage." Just going through certain religious practices such
as attending church, having family devotions, and being nice to each other

(at least in public) may have little meaning and integrity. They can never earn us the label "Christian," says Fairchild. "That description is given to us by him whose love we can only accept and make our own."

We build Christian family life as we work at communicating with each other. To understand ourselves we need to be understood by another person. "The quality of community, in the home and elsewhere," observes Fairchild, "depends upon the character of the communication among its members." In the previous week's devotions, we learned how crucial good communication, both verbal and nonverbal, is in marriage. The same is true in family living where children and other relatives are integral parts of family life. Being related by marriage or blood doesn't guarantee that we will communicate well.

The family can truly be a school for living. A Christian family can teach us how to love and forgive, how to listen and affirm others, how to give of ourselves unselfishly to another person. We build a Christian home as we play together, eat together (eating together is a bonding activity in all cultures), worship together around the meal table and in church, work together in and out of the home, suffer together, and share the dangers and anxieties that come to us all.

Christians in families affirm their unity, their commitment to one another to stay together "for better, for worse." This is another distinguishing mark of Christian family living. We affirm our unity despite our diversity. The key to such living is maturity through faith in God. Roy Fairchild writes:

> The mature person has learned to live comfortably with himself, knowing that he is adequate to do something useful in the world and that this is worth something to someone about whom he cares. For the Christian, that "someone" is supremely his Heavenly Father.

Christians in families are able to deal with their anger and conflict creatively. "Be angry but do not sin; do not let the sun go down on your anger, and do not make room for the devil" (Ephesians 4:26-27). No matter how much we like another person, there is always something about the other that can irritate us. When we get angry we need to "own" the feeling without acting destructively toward ourselves or others. There is *no* place for physical or emotional abuse of another person in Christian families. Counting to ten to "cool off," taking a walk, or punching a pillow can enable us to deal with anger without hurting another person. Being a Christian involves kindness, patience, and humility in our daily living.

A final mark of a Christian family is that it is *giving* in nature—giving not only to one another but to those outside the family. We build a Christian home as we give our money to others through church and charities. We express our Christian love as we give ourselves in volunteer service in the church and community. We give as Christ gave to us as we welcome visitors into our home for meals and visits. There are many people who live alone for whom a few hours with family are a high point. Families can become ingrown and selfish if they do not learn to give and continue to practice giving themselves and their possessions to others.

Prayer
Lord, help us to live as Christians in families, loving and forgiving one another as you have forgiven us. Teach us to give generously of ourselves to one another and to those outside our family circle. Amen. ❧

looking to the future

1. PLANNING FOR CHILDREN

When Esau looked up and saw the women and children, he said, "Who are these with you?" Jacob said, "The children whom God has graciously given your servant." (Genesis 33:5)

There is no greater thrill for a husband and wife who want children than to become parents. Elizabeth Achtemeier calls children "a marvelous superfluity, the frosting on our cake of matrimonial bliss!" While children are a gift God gives us, it is good to know that children are not necessary to a successful marriage. Most couples, however, do hope to become parents, and they need to plan ahead for this special responsibility.

Planning for children involves using our God-given judgment rather than leaving it to nature entirely. It is important for couples to discuss and agree upon methods of contraception, the number of children they would like to have, and the hoped-for interval between children. Our responsibility for subduing creation and having dominion over it must be balanced with God's command to Adam and Eve to "be fruitful and multiply" (Genesis 1:28).

Many marriage counselors and pastors advise newlywed couples to delay the first pregnancy for at least a year in order to build a stronger relationship before children arrive. The birth of the first child is a major crisis for many couples. The coming of children intensifies the existing state of a marriage. A happy marriage is usually made even happier, but an unhappy relationship usually only grows worse. The birth of the first child immediately creates a new community of three instead of two. In *Seasons of a Marriage,* Norman

Wright writes that being a parent can be compared to being an astronaut, says Wright. In spite of all the good training and information you are given, your own experience as a parent cannot be predicted. You are on an uncharted course. Being a parent is like swimming, adds Wright. "Some people plunge in without thinking and do a beautiful backstroke; others barely manage a 'survival float'; still others can't do even that. They have to call for help." All of us who are parents can attest to that!

One or both of you may be marrying again and bringing one or more children to your new family. This can be a source of joy as you form an "instant family" with "her" and/or "his" children. But problems can arise that will call for guidance from a pastor or family therapist. It is well to anticipate problems and to give extra attention to relationships and individuals as preventive measures. One of the secrets to parenting is a good marriage relationship and a commitment to unity that children of whatever age cannot destroy. When parents agree on discipline and other aspects of childrearing, more than half the battle is won.

Children are a gift from God through which God teaches us many things. From the moment a couple learns the wife is pregnant, they begin to learn new roles. When the baby is born and as he or she grows, parenting becomes more complex. Norman Wright explains why: (1) each parent is going through his or her own individual growth and change process; (2) the couple is working out their own relationship; and (3) if there is more than one child, parents have multiple parental roles.

Parents of one child proceed through their own adjustments progressively one step at a time, says Wright, but when a second or third child is added the roles and adjustments become even more complex. But by the grace of God and steadfast love for our children, we can be successful parents.

One of the things children teach us is *humility*. Before children arrive, a couple may think they are mature and self-controlled. But, as someone has said, children reinforce our belief in the reality of original sin! We become angry at our helpless infant who sleeps all day and cries all night or with older children who bicker and fight with one another. In *The Committed Marriage* Elizabeth Achtemeier observes:

> Somehow in relations with our children, we parents are brought face to face with our own terrible limitations—our inability always to love, to keep our tempers, to understand, to enter into another's viewpoint, to convince and guide by reason. We are brought quite existentially to confrontation with sinful depths in ourselves that we never knew existed. For a Christian, that can be

a very helpful experience, a signpost on the way to healing and personal wholeness.

In dealing with our children, we become more aware of the limits of our wisdom, and we discover that we cannot run our own lives alone but need God's wisdom and guidance and grace.

Being parents can also "greatly increase our self-respect and our knowledge of our own capacity for good and self-sacrifice," says Achtemeier. "We are faced with what has been called "manifold servitudes.'" We learn to do for children what they are unable to do for themselves. It is surprising how much service to our children prods us to greater maturity. "Our children call forth from us an astounding store of competence, maturity, and goodness. Our love for them enables us to become persons we never could have become had we not been required to serve their needs and rights," according to Achtemeier.

One final word about anticipating parenthood. There are excellent resources now to help couples gain the necessary skills for parenting. There are classes provided by community organizations and churches. Learn all you can before the baby comes, and have a network of friends and family to whom you can go for help and support. Having children can only be wonderful if you are good parents—and you will need all the help you can get!

Prayer
Lord, thank you for the gift of children. Bless our marriage with children according to your will. Amen.

2. STAGES OF GROWTH IN MARRIAGE

You were taught to put away your former way of life, your old self, corrupt and deluded by its lusts, and to be renewed in the spirit of your minds, and to clothe yourselves with the new self, created according to the likeness of God in true righteousness and holiness. (Ephesians 4:22-24)

For I want you to know how much I am struggling for you, . . . I want their hearts to be encouraged and united in love . . . (Colossians 2:1-2)

Life is an everflowing stream. We grow and mature as individuals and as our marriage relationship continues to unfold and develop. Our hearts are knit together in love and this love is a gracious gift from God. To *live* is to change and develop. This is what gives zest to life and keeps an edge on our relationship. To always know what the other one will do, to be so much in a

routine of daily habits that we take each other for granted is to invite boredom and disaster. In a successful marriage husband and wife continue to
grow and to mature.

Since money is such an important factor in every marriage, one way to
describe the stages of marriage is in terms of our financial situation at various
stages. If we have some understanding of the overall view of marriage and the
ways financial needs change as we advance in life, we will be better prepared
to cope satisfactorily. These transitions are described as four stages by Judson
and Mary Landis in *Building a Successful Marriage*:

- *Stage I.* This is a financial honeymoon period. In many cases both members
  of the pair are working and there may have been some parental subsidy or
  financial gift at the time of the wedding, as well as other wedding gifts. . . .
  Thus launched, and with two incomes, the average couple feels little financial pinch at first. They are inclined, under our present credit system, to be
  overly optimistic in the things they buy, basing their monthly ability to pay
  on their two incomes.
- *Stage II.* The first child is born and the wife may stop or cut down on the
  hours or days she works. . . . This stage, roughly ten years, when the couple
  is 25 to 35, is for many couples a period of financial strain approaching
  crisis. The husband's earning power is probably slowly increasing, but does
  not even approach the increase in expenses. . . . This is the stage in which
  the couple's ability to make their money go as far as possible is tested.
- *Stage III.* During the years from 35 to 45 the burden is still heavy but may
  begin to ease. At this stage the children are in school and the mother may
  begin to work again at least part-time to add to the family income.
- *Stage IV.* The years from 45 on, for the educated couple, are financially the
  easiest. . . . At this time they can concentrate more of their financial efforts
  upon investments that will ensure security for them in old age.

One of the values in taking an overview of the stages of married life and its
finances is that we get a better idea of the objectives of each stage in which
we find ourselves.

As newlyweds you are setting out on a journey together. You may be
young, in the middle years, or older. Whatever your age, as you journey
through life there is one thing that will make all the difference in your relationship: *commitment*. When you made your vows to each other, you
pledged to be faithful to each other "for better, for worse" as long as you live.

Commitment to God in Jesus Christ is the basis of a successful marriage at whatever stage. To love God and love our partner as we love ourselves brings a new dimension to marriage. God's steadfast love enables us to love and keep on loving.

In addition to the financial stages of marriage there are other seasons or stages. For couples who marry in their younger years the stages may go like this: the beginning of marriage; a season of dreams and expectations; children born or adopted; the season of mid-life; the empty nest; the golden years; a time to die. Each stage presents its unique opportunities for growth and its challenges. Each calls for flexibility, courage, and creativity in addition to commitment.

Norman Wright cites three reasons why marriages dissolve. The first is failure on the part of one or both partners to understand the stages and changes of marriage and how these affect the relationship. The second reason is that one or both partners build(s) her or his personal identity and security on an inadequate basis. And the third reason for marriage failure is unrealistic expectations about marriage.

We can find strength and guidance to work through each stage of marriage through prayer. Couples often find they can pray aloud with each other and express to God heartfelt repentance, joy, and thanksgiving—feelings that are often too difficult to express to their partner alone. Praying together draws on divine resources and brings us closer to the Creator who designed marriage as a structure of human society.

As you move through each stage of marriage you will find unique challenges that you never faced before and never anticipated. If you work at your marriage relationship and give it top priority in terms of time, energy, and thought, you can move through each stage successfully.

The Holy Spirit is God's presence and power that is available to us as we journey through life together. The Holy Spirit enables us to put off our old nature and to be renewed in the spirit of our minds. The spirit of God makes love real in our hearts and knits them together. We may unravel them at times with anger and sharp words and selfish deeds, but God's love continues to knit our hearts together and enables us to be faithful to one another.

Prayer
O God, thank you for life and growth. Thank you for knitting our hearts together in love. Help us to love one another more in each stage of marriage. Amen.

3. IN-LAWS AND OTHER FRIENDS

But Ruth said, "Do not press me to leave you or to turn back from following you! Where you go, I will go; where you lodge, I will lodge; your people shall be my people, and your God my God. Where you die, I will die—there will I be buried. . . ." When Naomi saw that she was determined to go with her, she said no more to her. (Ruth 1:16-18)

"I married you, not your family!" a young bride exclaimed when her husband suggested that they go to his parents' home for Sunday dinner each week as he had done before they were married. There is a sense, however, in which we do marry each other's family. A number of marriage ceremonies take this into account and include the parents of the bride and groom in the ceremony. In the first part of "A Service of Christian Marriage" of The United Methodist Church, parents or representatives of the families are invited to say to the couple: "We rejoice in your union, and pray God's blessing upon you." The minister asks the congregation (which includes in-laws and friends), "Will all of you, by God's grace, do everything in your power to uphold and care for these two persons in their marriage?" And they answer: "We will." The congregation is invited to affirm the couple by saying: "In the Name of Jesus Christ we love you. By his Grace, we commit ourselves with you to the bonds of marriage and the Christian home." Like it or not, marriage does create new relationships for us as bride and groom with our respective families and friends. Their wholehearted support and encouragement can help launch our new marriage on a successful voyage.

J. C. Wynn comments in *Family Therapy in Pastoral Ministry* (San Francisco: Harper & Row, 1982) that a whole group of family problems centers around marriage adjustments "that may occur in *early months of settling,* with relations to in-laws, with conflicts that grow through the years, with infidelities, or even breakdown and divorce." Families, whether just bride and groom or parents with several children, are *systems.* We can no longer think of ourselves as individuals or even as a couple separate from other persons. As Wynn points out:

> Once we gain the system perspective, we should no longer regard any person as an isolated individual apart from all others, but as one who belongs to a network of significant interrelationships. Each of us is a part of others in the context of a larger bundle of humankind.

The family system has power both to damage and build lives, and for this reason, we need to build good relations with our families.

The biblical story of Ruth and her devotion to her mother-in-law, Naomi, is a model of what family ties can mean to an individual. Ruth's words are sometimes incorporated into the wedding ritual for this reason. Writing in *Getting Ready for Marriage,* David Mace gives this counsel for avoiding needless in-law conflicts:

- No in-law interference can damage a sound marriage. . . . But any weakness, any crack in the unity of husband and wife, enables the in-laws to drive a wedge between them.

- The policy to adopt is to make it clear that you want to be friendly and to work for harmony between the generations, but that you simply will not tolerate unwarranted interference in your marriage. This must be made unmistakably clear and no compromise tolerated. Sometimes this can only be done in a painful, out-in-the-open, once-and-for-all confrontation. When the in-laws have thus been shown decisively that their interference will not be tolerated, they usually give up and accept the situation.

- This decisive confrontation should be followed up by sincere and genuine attempts to be friendly and conciliatory. . . . Many people make the mistake of thinking that if you have little in common with your in-laws, there is nothing you can do about it. In fact, you can behave lovingly even if you don't feel loving, and the action tends to promote the feeling. . . . Experience shows that this policy can in time achieve a surprising degree of success.

- If you and your in-laws really have very little in common, the best way to maintain good relationships is to visit them from time to time, but always keep the visits brief. . . . If you stay together too long with nothing much to do, tensions may arise and goodwill may deteriorate rapidly.

- Always remember that family ties cannot be broken, and last throughout a lifetime. . . . You cannot predict what the future will bring. The bonds that seem unimportant now may one day become a lifeline to you or to your children.

The first family challenge to peace in a new marriage is often a parent. Paradoxically, the problems may arise because family relationships are either too cool or too warm. As Ronna Romney and Beppie Harrison say in *Giving Time a Chance,* "Many marriages that work out well do start out with a perceptible coolness when it comes to relations with in-laws. On the other hand, for some couples the problem is that family relationships are too warm." Jesus, when questioned about divorce, said: "For this reason a man shall leave his father and mother and be joined to his wife, and the two shall become one flesh" (Matthew 19:5). "Leaving" one's parents calls for breaking emotional ties of dependency as well as leaving the parental home physically (if possible). Romney and Harrison point out that "The essential relationship, after all, is the one between husband and wife. It's nice if the whole extended family gets along, but it's crucial that the two of you do." The authors go on to say that some long-term marriages work only because one or both partners have become estranged from parents or family.

Friends are important. Engaged couples usually have close ties with other engaged or married couples. They also have single friends whose friendship is cherished after marriage. However, romantic ties to a friend should be terminated. Some wedding rituals include "forsaking all others" as a reminder that marriage is an exclusive relationship between a man and a woman. Like a private garden, marriage needs to be tended, watered, nourished, and given plenty of sunlight. But it also must be protected from intruders.

In order to get a better "feel" for the interaction with in-laws and friends, try the following exercise from *Family Therapy in Pastoral Ministry*:

> Stretching a clothesline from one person to others, we connect each person in that circle of five to each of the other four. This gives each a handful of four ropes, making a total of ten intertwining, tangled lines. When one pulls on any part of that rope it will tighten somewhere else. The others are affected at once by the tautness of the connection. No part of that entangled system is immune to tugs when any change is made in its slack or tightness. Despite the spaghetti-like tangle into which the demonstration sometimes collapses, the point becomes clear: everybody is connected.

Prayer
O God, who has created us to live in relationship, thank you for each person in our larger family and for our friends. Help us to be kind and considerate to one another, loving and forgiving, as you have loved and forgiven us. Amen.

4. SERVICE IN THE CHURCH AND COMMUNITY

You are the light of the world. A city built on a hill cannot be hid. No one after lighting a lamp puts it under the bushel basket, but on the lampstand, and it gives light to all in the house. In the same way, let your light shine before others, so that they may see your good works and give glory to your Father in heaven. (Matthew 5:14-16)

For you were called to freedom, brothers and sisters; only do not use your freedom as an opportunity for self-indulgence, but through love become slaves to one another. For the whole law is summed up in a single commandment, "You shall love your neighbor as yourself." (Galatians 5:13-14)

When I counsel with couples planning to be married, I emphasize the importance of their having a church relationship and giving themselves in community service. *Giving* is the best antidote to selfishness. Many of us have been blessed richly by our Christian heritage and by the communities in which we grew up. Teachers in church school, youth advisers, coaches, school teachers, pastors, and many other people have helped shape our lives. Now that we have reached this milestone in our lives, we have the privilege of sharing our strength and love with others.

The prayer of St. Francis is both a guide and inspiration to us as we seek ways to serve in the church and community:

> Lord, make me an instrument of your peace.
> Where there is hatred let me sow love.
> Where there is injury, pardon;
> Where there is doubt, faith;
> Where there is despair, hope;
> Where there is darkness, light; and
> Where there is sadness, joy.
> O divine Master, grant that I may not so much
> Seek to be consoled as to console;
> To be understood as to understand;
> To be loved as to love;
> For it is in giving that we receive;
> It is in pardoning that we are pardoned; and
> It is in dying that we are born to eternal life.

We seldom need to look very far to discover people who are hurting, who need help. In our daily work, in family and community gatherings, and in the church family we discover people who need our help and ways we can serve.

Jesus says that Christians are "the light of the world." In these early days of marriage we have so much love, joy, and hope, all of which the world desperately needs. "It is more blessed to give than to receive" (Acts 20:35) is relevant to our giving to those outside our immediate family as well as to family members. We are blessed by God as we share our lives with others rather than seeking only selfish pleasure and material comforts.

Elizabeth Achtemeier asks in *The Committee Marriage* if the final task of Christian marriage isn't that of being a "light to all in the house."

> Is it not only a lifelong vocation in which we wrestle and grow and learn and fight for our commitment to God and to each other, but it is also to be a light shining into the darkness of our society's homes? . . . We Christians finally bear witness to the world by how we live out our marital commitments. . . . By the way we conduct our marriages, we proclaim that Jesus Christ has won the victory over sin in the marital sphere too . . . for in the cross and resurrection of Jesus Christ is the healing for all our private hells.

We have been given the good news of Jesus' forgiving love. Now we are called to be ambassadors for Christ in a broken and needy world.

Many churches have church school classes for newly married couples, recognizing the special interests and needs they share in the early years of marriage. If your church does not have such a class, perhaps you would like to help start one. You might invite a few couples into your home for dessert and discussion of a special program for newly married people. Ask your pastor to join you to give the group guidance.

There are a number of programs designed to strengthen marriages. Ask your minister or a marriage counselor about such groups in your community. Newlyweds need a supportive community in which they can share their joys and concerns. The church is the ideal community to provide this. Also, community organizations such as YWCA, YMCA, mental health centers, and children and family service centers often offer classes in marriage and family life. As you join with other couples in strengthening your marriage and in enjoying fellowship with them, you will discover ways to help each other.

Many couples find meaningful service in the church through team teaching a church school class or working with youth. More churches are inviting couples to serve on committees, boards, and in other tasks as couples so that they may share their experiences of serving with each other.

When there are children from a previous marriage you may find your way of serving through programs in which your children are involved in the school and community. You may want to ask to serve in community organizations that help disadvantaged persons, elderly persons, or displaced persons.

Another way of serving is by giving money regularly to your church and to your favorite charities. We have many demands on our time and money, but each couple can discover particular community and worldwide programs that appeal to them. Make sure to research the ways charitable organizations manage their operations to assure that your donations are used for the purposes you intend. In serving others, we discover a deep inner satisfaction that selfish pleasures cannot give.

Prayer
Gracious God who has given us so much, help us discover ways to give to others more generously. Amen.

5. WEATHERING THE STORMS OF MARRIAGE

I have learned to be content, whatever the circumstances may be. I know how to live when things are difficult and I know how to live when things are prosperous. In general and in particular I have learned the secret of eating well or going hungry—of facing either plenty or poverty. I am ready for anything through the strength of the One who lives within me. (Philippians 4:11-13, Phillips)

In the name of God, I, (name), take you, (name),
to be my (wife) (husband),
to have and to hold from this day forward,
for better for worse, for richer for poorer,
in sickness and in health, to love and to cherish,
until we are parted by death. This is my solemn vow.
(From A Service of Christian Marriage*)*

During my college days I worked my passage to Israel on a cattle boat, feeding and watering mules and horses. We sailed along on calm seas most of the voyage, but sometimes the ship ran into rough seas and bobbed around on the waves like a cork. Since it was my first time at sea, I was frightened, wondering if the ship might split in half. Rumors spread by some of the older sailors that just such a calamity had happened to other ships did not help alleviate my fears! But the ship weathered the storms, and we arrived back in the U. S. A. intact.

Some years later when Sue and I were returning from a year of study in Scotland, our ship ran into rough weather in the North Atlantic. I was not as frightened as I was earlier on the cattle boat, because I knew we had made it through storms before. I was reassured on both trips by the knowledge that there was a captain in charge and he was directing the ship's course to bring us safely to harbor. Someone under his command was at the helm around the clock steering the ship.

On the voyage of matrimony we can expect to run into storms sooner or later. The vows we made earlier remind us that life is not all smooth sailing, but there are times when strong winds and high waves threaten to sink our little ship.

The steadfast nature of true love is expressed in these lines from "Sonnet 116" by William Shakespeare:

> Let me not to the marriage of true minds
> Admit impediments. Love is not love
> Which alters when it alteration finds,
> Or bends with the remover to remove.
> O, no! it is an ever-fixed mark
> That looks on tempest and is never shaken;
> It is the star to every wandering bark,
> Whose worth's unknown, although his height be taken.

We have promised to take each other as husband or wife "for better for worse, for richer for poorer, in sickness and in health." The most reassuring promise we have is that of Jesus: "I am with you always, to the end of the age" (Matthew 28:20). We are not alone on this voyage. The captain of the ship is none other than Jesus Christ!

The Apostle Paul gives the secret to weathering the storms of life in his letter to the Philippians when he writes: "I am ready for anything through the strength of the One who lives within me" (Philippians 4:13, Phillips). Life is very uncertain and unpredictable, but Christ's presence by the power of the Spirit is assured. Through prayer and reflection on Scripture, God will guide us safely through the roughest storms that may lie ahead.

The storms of life can draw us closer together as husband and wife or can drive a wedge between us. *Communication* is critical at these moments. If we can talk things over together, pray together, and get counsel from trusted friends and pastors we can usually "muddle through." There may be times we need the guidance and insights of a marriage counselor or family therapist to bring us safely to shore.

Commitment to stay together is another key factor in sailing successfully through storms. In our wedding vows we promised in these or similar words: "In the name of God I take you to be my (wife/husband) . . . to love and to cherish, until we are parted by death. This is my solemn vow." This commitment is based on our willpower, not on our romantic feelings. We are responsible for our decisions and must live with the consequences. Our commitment to stay married is like the compass at the ship's helm, which gives the captain his bearings in the storm. If we are bound and determined to make the marriage work, we are much more likely to succeed.

Christ in the body of the church can support us and guide us through the storms. When I was fired by a church earlier in my ministry, Sue and I found that a small group of loyal friends sustained us and guided us through one of the most distressing periods of our lives. "Bear one another's burdens, and in this way you will fulfill the law of Christ" (Galatians 6:2), writes Paul. He goes on to say "For all must carry their own loads" (Galatians 6:5). In other words, "Carry your own suitcases, but help each other with the heavy trunks!" We all have the little suitcase problems of everyday married life. We can and should cope with them as they come our way. But when we grapple with the trunks, with the big problems and disappointments, sorrows and trials, we need to help one another. We need to be humble enough to ask for help and let others take one end of our trunk! Christians are just such folk who "bear one another's burdens" and to whom we can turn in the storms of life.

Sue and I have found great joy in the friendship of an older couple with whom we have shared life's storms and successes through the years. They have been like a big sister and brother to us. I covet for you the friendship of older and younger couples as well as those your own age, for you will enrich each other's lives.

When things aren't going well in your marriage, the first place to look is at *yourself*. You are the only person you can change or control. You can free your partner to love you only as you make your partner feel loved. Marriage has been compared to gears that mesh. If they don't mesh, then look at yourself first. This is painful, but by the grace of God and with the help of trusted friends, pastors, and counselors, you can make it through. Sue and I had been married for twenty-three years when we discovered that, for the first time, we needed the counsel of a clinical psychologist. We learned to listen to each other more carefully and thus were helped through a difficult period in our marriage. Getting help *early*, before the relationship is damaged beyond repair, is crucial.

Prayer
Lord of love, come be the captain of our ship as we face together the storms that lie ahead. Give us courage to be steadfast in our vows to each other. Amen.

6. GOALS AND PLANS

Where there is no vision, the people perish. (Proverbs 29:18, KJV)

. . . but this one thing I do: forgetting what lies behind and straining forward to what lies ahead, I press on toward the goal for the prize of the heavenly call of God in Christ Jesus. (Philippians 3:13-14)

Some years ago I saw Jack Nicklaus make a hole-in-one at the Memphis Classic. It is said that Nicklaus practices putting so much that when the ball doesn't go in the hole, he is surprised. He has a clear goal, and when he doesn't achieve it, he is not just disappointed—he is surprised!

Marriage is a task that needs clearly defined goals if we expect to achieve success. Do you have a clear mental image of the kind of marriage you want to have twenty-five years from now? Or even on your next anniversary? If not, let me urge you to spend some time with your marriage partner talking over your hopes and dreams for your relationship.

Not all marriages are of the companionship type in which husband and wife are deeply involved in each other's lives. You have observed the marriages of your parents and friends and know the great variety of kinds of relationships that exist. In *Getting Ready for Marriage*, David Mace describes three kinds of marriages that you may want to consider as you discuss your own goals. The first kind is that of *minimum involvement*. "Husband and wife enter into a kind of agreement to meet each other's needs by an exchange of services. He promises to provide maintenance for her . . . She, for her part, agrees to be sexually available to him at all reasonable times, to run the home . . . and raise the children." I am sure you recognize that this kind of marriage is rather common. You may even know some people who have this kind of relationship.

A second kind of marriage reveals *maximum involvement* in which couples decide to share their lives as fully as possible. Mace says this kind of marriage "implies a decision to live together in complete openness and honesty with each other, to devote themselves to working together for the same life goals, to attach equal importance to the personal needs and vocational aims of both partners."

A third kind of marriage is characterized by *limited involvement*. In this style of marriage the partners "want to retain a good deal of individual freedom to go their own ways, but also they wish to enjoy a reasonable amount of togetherness. They want to give the marriage a worthy place among their commitments, but are not prepared to award it the top priority."

In his more recent book, *Close Companions* (New York: Continuum, 1982), Mace describes a fourth type of marriage that he calls *companionship marriage*:

> A socially registered commitment between a man and a woman, in which they seek to know themselves and each other as far as they are capable of being known, and, through mutual affection and affirmation, help each other to grow and change in order to become the loving and creative persons they are capable of becoming.

"Such a relationship requires courage and fortitude to accept the pain that such mutual self-disclosure may bring and that may be required for change as we grow," says Mace. He emphasizes that such a marriage can never cease to grow. Again, Mace says, "The product of a companionship marriage must be two loving and creative persons, . . . Any other goal must be considered secondary."

Our goals and plans for marriage nudge us to think through what we want to give to the relationship as well as what we want from it. All too often, however, couples have set goals only in terms of what they want *from* their marriage rather than what they intend to give *to* the marriage.

Some couples find it helpful to go away for a weekend to spend some time together. Released from the usual pressures of jobs and routines, we can dream dreams and see visions together. Vacations are another time for daydreaming about what we would like to have happen in the future.

The importance of positive mental imaging in order to replace destructive habits with good ones is being stressed in books on personal growth. A positive mental image of the kind of marriage you and your spouse want to achieve will give you a goal to strive toward. Reflect on the marriage models you know from observing couples you know. Share with each other what you like and don't like about the relationships as a way to shape the model you want as your goal.

You may want to list some of the goals and objectives you agree upon and then review them in a year. You may want to add to or change them, just as a ship's captain takes readings and corrects the course of the ship from time to time. If you find your ship going off course, then talk it over. Together, search for agreement on modifications of your original goals.

Some pastors invite couples to come in for "marriage checkups," just as dealers call in new automobiles for a 5,000 mile checkup. This can be very helpful, since a third party, like a pastor or marriage counselor, can assist you in reflecting on where you are in the relationship and how you would like to change it for the better. The first year of marriage is the *crucial* year. Your goals and plans for your marriage will enable you to work together to build a successful marriage.

Prayer
Lord, help us dream dreams together for the future of our relationship. Give us the courage and fortitude to make these dreams come true. Amen.

7. BE KIND TO ONE ANOTHER

. . . and be kind to one another, tenderhearted, forgiving one another, as God in Christ has forgiven you. (Ephesians 4:32)

Observers of marriages say that from a sociological point of view marriage is an almost impossible relationship. Two people of opposite sex, from different families, sometimes different races or nationalities, of different temperaments and sometimes widely different ages and experiences come together to live in the most intimate of relationships "until death do us part." A marriage counselor once commented that if we put difficulty in marriage on a scale of one to ten, with ten being the greatest difficulty, then marriage would be a fifteen!

This devotional guide is written primarily for couples recently married or for those planning to be married. It is designed to help couples build a healthy and successful relationship. Scripture tells us that God intends marriage to be a mutually fulfilling and forgiving relationship in which we are kind to one another. Unfortunately, not all partners fulfill this goal. Media reports tell us that abusive relationships are widespread. This abuse knows no social, economic, racial, religious, or educational boundaries. It is important to recognize abuse wherever it occurs, so that proper intervention can take place.

In domestic violence, eighty percent of abusers are men—twenty percent are women. Abuse can be both emotional and physical. The use of alcohol and drugs can release the restraints on anger and violence. Physical abuse is often inflicted on the abused where it cannot be seen. The abuser may become remorseful after the attack, begging forgiveness, promising never to abuse again, only to repeat the violence. This pattern of abuse can only be interrupted and corrected with professional intervention. While the ideal for marriage in Scripture is "until death do us part," it was never intended to mean death at the hand of an abusive spouse. Community agencies and some churches offer help and shelter for victims of domestic violence.

Being kind to one another takes on new meaning as we negotiate issues in the marriage relationship, rather than allowing one partner to dominate or seek to control the other. A maturing person is one who is willing and able to negotiate the day-to-day decisions required in any marriage. The marriage partnership implies a commitment to shared decision-making. As you begin to talk about finances, housing, jobs, and goals, there will many opportunities to show kindness toward one another. The act of *listening* to one another has already been emphasized in earlier chapters, but it is so crucial in building a successful marriage. If we truly care about our partner, we must be willing to listen to our partner's feelings and issues. Listening can be painful and difficult as we allow ourselves to become vulnerable in the process of maturing as individuals and as a couple.

In a practical sense, being kind is a matter of treating your partner as you would like to be treated. Be thoughtful of one another. Remembering birthdays, anniversaries, and other special events are important. These remembrances need not be extravagant to be meaningful. It may be necessary to remind each other of special days. Words of love and kindness are always appropriate. "I love you" is a message that never wears out! "I'm sorry, please forgive me" can never be said too often. Little surprises or an unanticipated phone call/email is a nice way to let your spouse know you are thinking about them. When your mate has experienced illness, disappointment, or loss, you will want to be especially thoughtful and supportive. Likewise, when one has achieved special recognition, words of celebration and congratulations are called for. A friend once said that we should be as nice to one another as we would be to guests in our home.

Prayer
Loving God, thank you for bringing us together. Thank you for loving us and forgiving us. Help us to love and forgive one another. Help us to be kind to one another. Amen. ❧

further reflections on marriage

1. NEGOTIATING CHORES

Bear one another's burdens, and in this way you will fulfill the law of Christ. .
. . For all must carry their own loads. (Galatians 6:2, 5)

In week 3, chapter 4, we looked at work in and out of the home. In today's world, in increasingly more households, both the husband and wife are working outside of the home. Sociologists tell us that household chores are one of the major sources of conflict in marriage. As newlyweds, you will want to start your marriage with an understanding about chores. No one can dictate how a couple will manage household chores. There are many models, and no doubt many couples simply follow patterns established in the families they came from. There is the traditional model of the wife as the person who takes care of all the household chores—cleaning, cooking, chauffeuring children, shopping, and laundry—and the husband takes care of house repairs, auto maintenance, and yard work. A more recent model is one of sharing chores because both the wife and husband work outside the home. In some marriages, there is a totally different model of the "househusband" who does the usual household chores while the wife is the primary or sole wage earner. For couples who can afford it, household chores are done by someone hired for that purpose. Any of these models can work well for some couples or none of them work well for others. Figuring out a plan that works for your marriage will depend on your individual abilities, resources, and preferences—and on some creative and loving negotiations.

We can all laugh at a recent cartoon with the man sitting in the easy chair in front of the television. His wife is standing nearby and says, "I think we should switch household chores for a while. You do all the cooking, cleaning, and laundry and I'll sit around on my butt and watch TV." No one wants to shoulder the brunt of the work while someone else enjoys their leisure. Who does what in and around the house and when does it get done?

The most obvious way to look at chores is to list them all—both in and out of the house, and an approximate time it takes to do each chore. Where possible, match chores with individual preferences of the couple (and later with children) and then negotiate the remaining chores as fairly as possible. It is also helpful to note when each chore should be completed. There will be some chores that people really want to do, and others that no one wants to do. Make sure that everyone gets some of both. Put the plan in operation for a certain period of time and then reevaluate the plan and adjust assignments as needed.

There may be times in a marriage when, due to illness or job demands, chores fall primarily on one person. A sense of humor can certainly help ease the tension of such times, but couples must be realistic and face the fact that some chores simply may not get done. There will be times when you will need help from family and friends. We had such a time when I was severely injured in an auto wreck and have been incapacitated with permanent disabilities since. Friends helped in so many ways. One friend who had experienced similar circumstances earlier and knew what we were going through did all our grocery shopping for us for many months. Many others prepared meals for us. One friend stayed with me when Sue's job required travel out of town. Our adult children and their spouses still help us with major tasks. When help is needed, accept it graciously and know that someday you will be able to help someone else in need.

James Thornton, the author of *Chore Wars*, tells of doing all the chores when his wife, Debbie, was confined to bed while pregnant with their second child. Thornton suddenly had to learn to cook, do the laundry, and care for their four-year-old son. He tells about keeping notes in a little book about how to do certain tasks and where to find items in the grocery store.

One newlywed couple who really felt like they did not know what was involved in regular housecleaning, nor how to go about it, did a creative thing. They could not afford a regular housecleaning service, but they had the service for one time only, watched carefully what those persons did and how they did it, and then tackled the job themselves.

You need not let traditional gender roles force you or your spouse into chores that are not ones you can do or that you like to do. At the same time, don't let gender roles keep you from doing a chore you really like. We all know men who are wonderful cooks and enjoy cooking. Many men do all or most of the shopping for the household groceries, furnishings, and much of the family's clothing. We know a busy wife who had a full-time house-keeper/cook, but the wife did the yard work, because she really liked to do so. She was often chided about this because she had three strapping sons who could have done the mowing. We only have to look around us to see many creative ways to get the chores completed. Some families will even admit that they enjoy chore time when everyone is working to get the job done—they feel a great sense of satisfaction when the chores are finished.

And finally, praise and affirmation go a long way in making chores less of a *chore!* Plan an outing or an event after chores, so that there is something to look forward to when the job is done.

Prayer
Loving God, we give you thanks for giving us work do with health and strength to do it. Forgive us when we complain about the chores of life. Give us grace to be cheerful and diligent as we go about the work of making our home clean and comfortable. Amen.

2. MARRYING AGAIN

. . . the fruit of the Spirit is love, joy, peace, patience, kindness, generosity, faithfulness, gentleness, and self control. . . . And those who belong to Christ Jesus have crucified the flesh with its passions and desires. (Galatians 5:22-24)

As you enter a new marriage there are a number of issues that have already been addressed or will need to be addressed soon. Whether your previous marriage ended by death or divorce, you will need help in healing from the experience so that you can make a new beginning. If the marriage ended by death, good grieving needs to occur in order for you to move on in life. The good and the not-so-good of that marriage need to be acknowledged, knowing that this new marriage will have some elements of both good and difficult times as well. If the former marriage ended in divorce, the elements of the divorce need to be looked at honestly, forgiven, and "put away" so that you may enter this new relationship on a solid foundation. Many churches and community agencies have programs to help in the specific areas of grief and divorce.

It will be important for each of you to look at the financial assets you bring to this marriage and decide how those assets will be maintained. If one or both of you have children, that will influence how those assets are handled. Many couples work out prenuptial agreements related to their assets so that each partner enters the marriage with full knowledge of the financial arrangements. If one or both of you have been living on your own for a time, it may be an adjustment to mesh the gears of your finances. Money matters, if not handled well, can be a cause for serious problems in the new marriage. Studies show that unresolved money issues and child-related issues are equally stressing and are the most prevalent causes for the breakup of a second marriage. There is a valuable resource for dealing with finances in a second marriage: *Money Advice for Your Successful Remarriage* by Patricia Schiff Estes. The subtitle is "Handling Financial Issues with Love and Understanding." The key words are *love* and *understanding*.

If there are children involved in this remarriage, helping them become a part of the new family will be a major undertaking before and in the early days of the marriage. Depending on the age and vulnerability of the children, you and your spouse will want to have a clear understanding of each other's parenting styles and goals for your children. You will want to acknowledge that these children may have some unresolved feelings about this marriage that need to be heard with love and understanding and that all members of the new family will get the help needed to resolve these issues. Remember that children are children, and that adults are expected to bring the maturity and understanding to the new relationships. These new relationships will take some time and much love.

There will be all the other issues of marriage to work out along with the ones mentioned above. You have a large challenge ahead, but you are not alone. God's love and spirit will be there for you through prayer, worship, fellowship with other couples in similar situations, and in counseling. Enjoy and affirm each other often. Make and take time just for the two of you when possible.

As we try to make sense of the various events and relationships of our lives, we may wonder what it all means. A poem by an anonymous author has been helpful to me, and I want to share it with you.

> The Weaver
> My life is but a weaving
> Between the Lord and me.
> I may not choose the colors;
> He knows what they should be;
> For He can view the pattern
> Upon the upper side

While I can see it only
On this, the under side.

Sometimes He weaveth sorrow,
Which seemeth strange to me;
But I will trust His judgment
And work on faithfully.
'Tis He who fills the shuttle,
And He knows what's best;
So I shall weave in earnest,
Leaving to Him the rest.

Not till the loom is silent
And the shuttles cease to fly
Shall God unroll the canvas
And explain the reason why
The dark threads are as needed
In the Weaver's skillful hand
As the threads of gold and silver
In the pattern He has planned.

Prayer
Gracious God, who has led us in the past, guide us as we are moving into the future. We trust in you to be our God when we cannot see the pattern of our lives, but we know that you can see it and you will care for us. Amen.

3. CONCLUSION

Then Jesus told his disciples, "If any want to become my followers, let them deny themselves and take up their cross and follow me. For those who want to save their life will lose it, and those who lose their life for my sake will find it." (Matthew 16:24-25)

It is more blessed to give than to receive. (Acts 20:35)

Some spouses introduce their partners to strangers by saying, "I want you to meet my *best friend.*" The lover in the Song of Solomon says of her beloved: "His speech is most sweet, and he is altogether desirable. This is my beloved and this is my friend, O daughters of Jerusalem" (Song of Solomon 5:16).

Certainly our spouse is a different kind of friend than our other friends, but a successful marriage is based on genuine friendship, a growing relationship between two people who are committed to each other for life.

Friends thank God for each other, for they recognize that the love uniting them is a gift from God. The attitude of thanksgiving is closely related to faith in God. To be thankful is to be "think-full," to think about our relationship to God and to one another. My mother married my father when they were in their mid-thirties. They were *grateful* for each other. This was one of their secrets to their joyful life and the success of their marriage of fifty-six years. George Herbert has expressed this spirit in "Our Prayer":

> Thou hast given so much to me,
> Give one thing more—a grateful heart;
> Not thankful when it pleaseth me,
> As if Thy blessing had spare days;
> But such a heart, whose pulse may be
> Thy praise.

To thank God for our spouse each day and to praise God with each heartbeat means living in constant communion with God.

Sue and I discovered that one of the secrets of getting through the storms is to *praise God* especially when things are not going well. We cannot honestly thank God for sickness, disappointment, frustration, or the death of a loved one. But we can praise God for the goodness, the care, and the comfort of God in all circumstances.

> Praise the Lord!
> O give thanks to the Lord,
> for he is good;
> for his steadfast love
> endures forever.
> (Psalm 106:1)

When a spouse is fired from a job or we are disappointed in not getting a promotion at work, we are likely to be angry and resentful. But if we can praise God and rejoice in God's goodness, we are released from feeling alone.

The quality of love that will sustain our marriage relationship and knit our hearts together, whatever may come our way, is the "steadfast love" of God that "endures forever." In our marriage vows we have committed ourselves to love one another as long as we both shall live. Feelings vary with our health, stress, and biorhythms as well as with stages in our life. We live in a stressful society and all too often let stress dull our emotions. Although we may feel emotionally wrung out, or bored, or angry, our commitment to stay together "for better, for worse" can see us through these periods of life. God's steadfast love remains constant, and God's love knits our hearts together by the power of the Spirit.

Building a successful marriage, like any other task, takes constant effort. There are times when we need to work at the relationship more than other times, but we should never take our partner or our relationship for granted. Boredom due to frustration and poor communication invites disaster. Both partners must work at keeping the sparkle in the relationship.

Throughout these devotionals you have noticed certain themes that reappear like phrases in a piece of music. *Communication* is one of those themes. Couples who are building a successful marriage (and it is an ongoing process rather than a static achievement) are able to communicate both verbally and nonverbally with each other. They have learned to listen creatively—to really hear what the other person is saying. Marriage partners can relate to each other as best friends. The importance of *friendship* in marriage is a theme you have noted throughout this book. *Developing a caring attitude* in marriage is another recurring theme. It is important that our partner perceives that we care deeply. We like to be told "I love you" and we expect this to be demonstrated in actions also. In a very happy marriage, each partner accepts the other partner. We forgive the other for the hurts caused us and we accept him or her in spite of shortcomings and faults. We can do this only by the grace of God who accepts us and enables us to accept others freely. *Forgiveness* is basic to a lasting and growing relationship. Finally, marriage is a process that involves renewing our vows of *commitment* to each other.

Our daughter had a poster of a kitten hanging from a tree limb by its front paws. The caption read: "Hang in There, Baby!" To each of you as you begin your marriage I say: "Hang in there!" By the grace of God and with your commitment to build a successful marriage, you can experience one of the greatest gifts of God to any man or woman—the joy of a very happy marriage.

Prayer
The Lord bless you and keep you;
the Lord make his face to shine upon you, and be gracious to you;
the Lord lift up his countenance upon you, and give you peace.
(Numbers 6:24-26) ❦

suggestions for further reading

Bazerman, Max H. *Smart Money Decisions.* New York: John Wiley & Sons, Inc, 1999.

Biddle, Perry H. *A Marriage Manual.* Grand Rapids: Eerdmans, 1994.

Brouwer, Douglas J. "What Christians Believe about Marriage" in *Beyond "I Do."* Grand Rapids: Eerdmans, 2001.

Coleman, Paul. *The 30 Secrets of Happily Married Couples.* Holbrook MA: Bob Adams, Inc. Publishers, 1992.

Estess, Patricia Schiff. "Handling Delicate Finnancial Issues with Love and Understanding" in *Money Advice for Your Successful Remarriage.* Cincinnati: Betterway Books, 1996.

Gottman, John M. "A Practical Guide from the Country's Foremost Relationship Expert" in *The Seven Principles for Making Marriage Work.* New York: Crown Publishers, Inc., 1999.

Huffman, Jennifer Lee. "Choices, Rights and Responsibilities" in *Money and Marriage.* Petoskey MI: Torch Lake Publishing, 1998.

Liberman, Gail and Alan Lavine. "Understanding and Achieving Financial Compatibility Before-and-After You Say 'I Do'" in *Love, Marriage and Money.* Chicago: Dearborn Financial Publishing, Inc., 1998.

Lueking, F. Dean. "A Guide for Couples Preparing to Marry" in *Let's Talk Marriage.* Grand Rapids: Eerdmans, 2001.

Mack, Dana and David Mack, eds. "The Wisest Answers to the Toughest Questions" in *The Book of Marriage.* Grand Rapids: Eerdmans, 2001.

Mellan, Olivia. "Resolving Money Conflicts in Your Life and Relationships" in *Money Harmony.* New York: Walker Publishing Company, Inc., 1994.

Orman, Suze. "Practical and Spiritual Steps So You Can Stop Worrying" in *The 9 Steps to Financial Freedom.* New York: Crown Publishers, Inc., 1997.

Shimer, John C. "A User-friendly Guide for Engaged Couples and Newlyweds About How to Make Dreams Come True Through Successful Money Management" in *Secrets to Financial Success in Marriage.* Kirkland WA: Successful Financial Planners, Inc., 1992.

Thornton, James. "How Households Can Share the Work & Keep the Peace" in *Chore Wars.* Berkeley CA: Conari Press, 1997.

Wangerin Jr., Walter. "Crafting Your Marriage to Last" in *As for Me and My House.* Nashville: Thomas Nelson Publishers, 1990.

where to turn when you need help

When you need supportive counseling, you may want to talk it over with your pastor. She or he may be able to refer you to a licensed pastoral counselor. Or you may look in the phone book for Licensed Marriage and Family Therapists. Another resource is the American Association of Pastoral Counselors.

American Association of Pastoral Counselors
9504-A Lee Highway
Fairfax, VA 22031-2303
Phone: 703-385-6967
Email: info@aapc.org

You may use the website below to get names of licensed pastoral counselors in your area.

www.aapc.org